The Complete SODA MAKING BOOK

FROM HOMEMADE ROOT BEER TO SELTZER AND SPARKLERS,

100 Recipes to Make Your Own Soda

JILL HOUK

Published by
Adams Media, a division of F+W Media, Inc.
57 Littlefield Street, Avon, MA 02322. U.S.A.
www.adamsmedia.com

Chapter 12 contains material adapted and abridged from *The Big Book of Slow Cooker Recipes* by Rachel Rappaport, copyright © 2013 by F+W Media, Inc., ISBN 10: 1-4405-6069-2, ISBN 13: 978-1-4405-6069-9; *The Big Book of Vegetarian Recipes* by Rachel Rappaport, copyright © 2013 by F+W Media, Inc., ISBN 10: 1-4405-7257-7, ISBN 13: 978-1-4405-7257-9; *The Everything® Busy Moms' Cookbook* by Susan Whetzel, copyright © 2013 by F+W Media, Inc., ISBN 10: 1-4405-5925-2, ISBN 13: 978-1-4405-5925-9; *The Everything® Cake Mix Cookbook* by Sarah K. Sawyer, copyright © 2009 by F+W Media, Inc., ISBN 10: 1-60550-657-5, ISBN 13: 978-1-60550-657-9; and *The Everything® Giant Book of Juicing* by Teresa Kennedy, copyright © 2013 by F+W Media, Inc., ISBN 10: 1-4405-5785-3, ISBN 13: 978-1-4405-5785-9.

ISBN 10: 1-4405-6748-4
ISBN 13: 978-1-4405-6748-3
eISBN 10: 1-4405-6749-2
eISBN 13: 978-1-4405-6749-0

Printed in the United States of America.

10 9 8 7 6 5 4 3 2 1

Library of Congress Cataloging-in-Publication Data

Houk, Jill.
  The complete soda-making book / Jill Houk.
     pages cm
  Includes bibliographical references and index.
  ISBN 978-1-4405-6748-3 (pbk. : alk. paper) -- ISBN 1-4405-6748-4 (pbk. : alk. paper) -- ISBN 978-1-4405-6749-0 (eISBN) -- ISBN 1-4405-6749-2 (eISBN)
  1. Soft drinks. 2. Syrups. 3. Fruit drinks. I. Title.
  TP630.H68 2014
  641.2'6--dc23

                    2013033178

Always follow safety and commonsense cooking protocol while using kitchen utensils, operating ovens and stoves, and handling uncooked food. If children are assisting in the preparation of any recipe, they should always be supervised by an adult.

This book is available at quantity discounts for bulk purchases. For information, please call 1-800-289-0963.

To my son, Sam, who is my reason for making homemade sodas that are healthier and more eco-friendly than what's available in stores.

ACKNOWLEDGMENTS

Many thanks to the manufacturers whose representatives and public relations agents provided me with information about their products. Their time and knowledge helped me understand the carbonation process, and guided me as I developed recipes that work well with in-home carbonators.

Another round of thanks goes to my family. Great appreciation goes to my cousin, Adrienne Jaycox, one of the earliest adopters of at-home carbonation. Her enthusiasm about making sparkling beverages in her home got the rest of the family primed to try the process for ourselves. Also thank you to my parents, Rick and Donna Yule, who bought my first at-home carbonation system.

Thanks to Lois Weinblatt, along with her parents, Howard and Judy Weinblatt, and my son Sam, for their tireless recipe testing and advice on how to adjust each recipe. Their palates stayed fresh despite hours of drinking batch after batch of soda.

And, finally, endless appreciation to my husband, Scott Herrington, who encourages and supports me in more ways than I have space to mention.

Contents

INTRODUCTION

Even a few years ago, the thought of making your own club soda and carbonated drinks at home seemed daunting. However, with recent popularity of at-home carbonators (from manufacturers such as SodaStream, Cuisinart, and iSi), times have changed, and many home gourmets are not only making sparkling water at home; they are also experimenting with their own versions of colas, fruit sodas, and unusual sodas, such as herbal drinks.

And with good reason! Not only can you save money by making your own sparkling beverages at home; you can also control exactly what goes into your drinks, and lessen your environmental impact. And, most importantly, you can pick up a fun new hobby! In addition, home soda-making goes hand-in-hand with home mixology. If you're investing in making craft cocktails at home, take it a step further by creating your own carbonated mixers.

Once you master a few simple principles, making sparkling beverages at home is quick and easy. Using this book as a guide, you'll be an expert in no time. First, begin by reading Part 1, with some background information, descriptions of at-home carbonators (which also include handy guidelines for choosing the carbonator that's right for you), and recommendations for other kitchen tools needed for making your own sodas. Next, you'll see just how easy it is to master the basics of home carbonation, store your flavored bases, and fix any problems that might arise. Then, you'll be ready to dive into the recipes. In Part 2, you'll find everything from replicas of store-bought colas, root beers, and ginger ales, to fruit sodas, to unusual combinations such as pineapple cilantro soda or soda with lavender.

In Part 3, you'll use the sodas you know how to make to create other drinks and even foods! You'll find nonalcoholic options, such as a Shirley Temple or a spooky bubbling punch (perfect for Halloween!), and delicious cocktails, like the Old-Fashioned, the Dark and Stormy, and the unique Sparkling Cosmopolitan. And, finally, if you're getting hungry, the last section contains recipes for foods—like Cola-Brined Fried Chicken or Strawberry Soda Pop Cake—which also rely on homemade soda pop as an ingredient.

So what are you waiting for? These bubbles aren't going to hang around forever. Let's get reading and cooking!

Part 1

AN OVERVIEW OF CARBONATION

Everyone can name their favorite fizzy beverage. Whether it's plain sparkling water, store-bought root beer, or a homemade peach soda, we all have a sparkling drink that we call our "own." Few of us, however, can explain why certain drinks are fizzy, or explain the magic of carbonation. Luckily, carbonation is a simple concept with an interesting history. The following chapters explain what carbonation is, and tell you how it went from a natural phenomenon to an everyday, at-home process.

CHAPTER 1

Carbonating 101

In this chapter, you'll learn about the background of carbonation—what it is, its history, and why you'd want to carbonate water at home.

What Is Carbonation?

Carbonation is the suspension of a gas called carbon dioxide in a liquid. It's the bubbly part of club soda, soda pop, champagne, or beer. A form of carbonation also occurs in bread (it's what helps bread rise) and cheese (such as Swiss cheese, in which carbonation is responsible for the holes). Carbon dioxide stays dissolved in water under pressure, and when pressure is released, it separates into small gas bubbles. Tightly closed bottles of carbonated beverages appear not to have bubbles in them because they're under pressure. As soon as you open them, you reduce the pressure, releasing the carbon dioxide from the liquid and creating the bubbles we all know and love.

CARBONATION IN NATURE

The first examples of carbonation occurred naturally. Some mineral springs naturally have carbon dioxide dissolved in water, resulting in effervescent waters. Examples of natural springs are Les Bouillens Springs in France (the source of Perrier sparkling water), as well as Poland Spring and Garden Spring in the town of Poland, Maine (the source of Poland Spring bottled water). These springs were formed when carbon dioxide gas became trapped within the springs' rocks during formation. As water encountered the carbon dioxide, it became bubbly. Waters from these springs were (and are still!) bottled and sold as health tonics.

CARBONATION WITH YEAST

Another type of natural carbonation occurs with yeast—a microscopic, one-celled fungus. Yeast naturally exists in the air, in soil, in water, and on most surfaces. Yeast feeds on simple sugars, which are abundantly found in fruit. Thousands of years ago, yeast landed in fruit juice, consumed the sugars in the juice, and left behind byproducts of alcohol and carbon dioxide. Some early carbonated beverages resulted when juice and yeast were placed together into airtight containers. Initially, this process was a happy accident, but once the process was discovered, it was refined by the Romans, and people have been able to create carbonation themselves by adding yeast to juice. The yeast consumed the sugar in the juice, and created alcohol and carbon dioxide. Because they were together in a closed container, the carbon dioxide dissolved in the juice, creating carbonation. The carbonation was detected once the containers were opened and bubbles appeared.

EARLY COMMERCIAL CARBONATION

In the eighteenth century, Joseph Priestley, a British chemist and theologian, learned how to make carbonated water by infusing water with the air found in breweries above fermentation tanks. At roughly the same time, a Swedish chemist and mineralogist, Torbern Bergman, discovered how to carbonate water using similar methods. Later in that same century, German-born Swiss watchmaker J.J. Schweppe created a commercial process for carbonation based on Priestley's and Bergman's methods.

EARLY AT-HOME CARBONATION

Carbonation became possible at home in the mid-nineteenth century with the introduction of siphons, canisters that hold water and allow it to be carbonated by a single-use small carbon dioxide charger. Shortly thereafter, in the early twentieth century, devices were created that allowed consumers to carbonate bottles of water using larger carbon dioxide carbonators. These carbonators could carbonate up to 30 liters of water per carbonator. At-home carbonators were typically used in bars, and in the homes of upper-class families, and were more common in Europe than in North America. Some of the current at-home carbonator brands, such as iSi and SodaStream, can trace their starts as far back as the early twentieth century.

Nowadays, at-home carbonators are readily available to consumers, with manufacturers selling a range of products to suit every consumer's budget, need for portability, and decor.

Why Carbonate at Home?

Why should you make your own sparkling beverages when there are so many terrific bubbly waters and sodas available in local grocery stores? There are several reasons for going the do-it-yourself route. Not only is at-home carbonation and soda-making fun; it is easy on the pocketbook, affords the most flexibility for creating your favorite flavors, and is better for the planet.

IT'S LESS EXPENSIVE

First, at-home carbonation can be economical. When you consider that the least expensive sparkling water you can buy in a store is roughly 75 cents per liter, you definitely save money by making your own sparkling water. Most municipalities sell water for less than one cent per gallon. Even when you consider the cost of the carbonation device (devices have a starting price of $80 and have enough supplies to make your initial 60 liters of sparkling water) and the cost of refilling CO_2 chargers (typically around $15 for 60 liters of water), the cost of making sparkling water at home comes out to approximately 50 cents per liter (assuming you make at least 240 liters with your machine). Once you reach this initial amount of consumption (which can take anywhere from nine months to a year, if you have a liter of water per day), the cost of each liter of water is roughly 25 cents per liter.

Making flavored sparkling drinks at home does cost more than sparkling water. Large-scale commercial soft drink manufacturers are able to buy ingredients in bulk and process them inexpensively, often resulting in a store-bought product that is less expensive than making soda at home. However, if you have a surplus of fruit from your garden, or find a bargain on produce or spices, your costs to make soda at home will be substantially less.

Where you will see real economic value in making your own soda is if you compare the cost of homemade soft drinks against the cost of *artisanal, all-natural* commercial drinks. At the store, soft drinks that are free from chemicals and dyes, and made from sugar and real fruit, can cost upwards of $5 per liter. In comparison, making a liter of all-natural soda at home is less than half that cost! If you don't live in an area where you can buy all-natural sodas in your local store, you will also have to pay for shipping commercial products to your home, making it even more economical to make soda yourself.

CONTROLLING FLAVORS AND INGREDIENTS

Another great reason to carbonate at home is to control exactly what ends up in your sparkling beverages. With prepackaged soft drinks, the manufacturer decides everything about the drink: the ingredients, the concentration, the level of carbonation. Making your own drinks will allow you to decide all of those factors and more. You can:

- Create soft drinks from all-natural and/or organic ingredients
- Base your soft drinks on whatever ingredients you find cheaply or in abundance
- Use ingredients you grow in your garden
- Control the sugar or sweetener in each drink

- Carbonate your sodas to the point where you can barely detect the bubbles, or to the point where you can't take a sip without the sparkles tickling your nose
- Discover delicious flavor combinations you can't find in stores

In short, flexibility and creative control are the best reasons to make your own carbonated drinks at home.

ENVIRONMENTAL IMPACT

Finally, you might make sparkling beverages at home to lessen your impact on the environment. When you make your own sparkling soft drinks, you use sturdy, reusable bottles, thereby eliminating the need for single-use plastic bottles, glass bottles, cartons, and cans. Often these containers wind up in landfills or waterways. Even if you were to recycle every single bottle, carton, and can you used, a tremendous amount of energy goes into the recycling process, and only a fraction of the recycled materials go into new beverage containers. (Some of the recycled materials do end up as other items, like jackets or decorative containers.) By carbonating at home, you reduce the need to manufacture soda containers.

There is also an environmental impact associated with transportation when you use disposable bottles, cans, and cartons. When you buy carbonated drinks at the store, you're using gasoline to get to and from the store. In addition, the manufacturer is using gas to bring the drinks to your grocer's in the first place. It's likely that your drink was created in a processing plant thousands of miles away from your store, which means it had to travel that distance, using fossil fuels to get there. You don't need as much transportation when you make your own sodas. You can simply walk to your sink, fill your bottle with water, and carbonate.

> ## Traveling Out to Buy Ingredients
>
> Even if you are expending fuel to go to the store and buy ingredients for flavorings, the environmental impact is minimal. Even better—walk or take your bike to the store! The ingredients you'll need are usually not very large or heavy.

Other Uses for Carbonation

In addition to making club soda and other sparkling drinks, you'll find carbonated water is useful in many situations:

- In baked goods, carbonation creates an airier, more tender product. In fact, you'll find recipes in this book for pancakes, waffles, and cakes that contain homemade club soda.
- Carbonated water is an excellent fabric cleaner. The effervescence helps to remove stains from fabrics. Simply douse a stain with carbonated water, let sit for ten minutes, and then launder as usual.

- Soda water is a great way to clean countertops and porcelain surfaces. Pour a little club soda onto the area you'd like to clean, and wipe the soda away.
- Soda water is a great jewelry cleaner. Soak your jewelry in a glass of club soda overnight to remove mineral deposits and oils, and leave your gems as sparkling as the water you soaked them in.

The question really is, why *not* make your sparkling water at home? Read on to discover what kinds of equipment you need to get the job done.

CHAPTER 2

Equipment You'll Need

Making soft drinks at home has become increasingly popular due to the widespread sale of carbonators and carbon dioxide chargers. In this chapter, you'll learn the basics of at-home carbonation systems, as well the other kitchen tools you need to become an expert in home soda-making.

Choosing a Carbonator

Many factors go into choosing the best carbonator for your needs. You'll need to think about:

- Where you intend to store your device (countertop or elsewhere)
- Your budget
- Whether you need a portable device
- How often you'd like to buy chargers (more on chargers in a bit)
- Whether you have had a good or not-so-good experience with a manufacturer's other products
- Your decor

Learning a little bit about the different styles before you buy will help ensure that you find the machine that's right for you.

Types of Carbonators

In general terms, the devices you use to carbonate beverages at home can be broken down into three categories: siphons, stand-up carbonation systems, and bottle-cap carbonators.

SIPHONS

The Low-Down on Siphons:

- Siphons are canisters with a mechanism for releasing carbonation into a liquid contained in the canister.

- The cartridges sold for siphons are single-use only. You can buy the cartridges in bulk at housewares stores, and online.
- The best-known brand for siphons is iSi, which has been making European-manufactured siphons since 1867.
- Siphons have a price range from $80 to $110.

Siphons are metal canisters, either aluminum or stainless steel, that have a screw-top with a mechanism for releasing carbon dioxide or nitrous oxide (also known as laughing gas) into the liquid contained in the canister. They are sold with chargers, which are small cartridges that contain pressurized carbon dioxide or nitrous oxide. To operate, you fill the siphon with water, close the cap tightly, add a charger, and screw the charger casing in tightly to release the gas from the charger into your liquid. You then dispense your carbonated beverage from the siphon.

Siphons are fairly small in size. For that reason, you can store siphons in a cabinet, or on a tall shelf. Their size makes them portable, meaning you can take them anywhere you'd like carbonated beverages, such as picnics and parties. Most siphons have an elegant appearance and are intended for display, coming in a variety of colors. These siphons look terrific on top of home bars, alongside metal cocktail shakers and ice buckets.

Two types of siphons exist.

1. **Those made for water:** These can carbonate only unflavored, plain water. Other liquids (such as flat soda) will clog the mechanism and leave behind residue that can decay and ruin the siphon.

   - **Pro:** Water siphons have a down spout that makes it easy to pour carbonated water into glasses or pitchers
   - **Con:** You can't use it for any type of flavored liquids.

2. **Those made for other liquids:** This type of siphon was originally made for turning heavy cream into whipped cream, but can be used for a multitude of other purposes. For example, you can use these siphons to carbonate plain water, or carbonate water that has base added. You can also carbonate whole pieces of fruit, or use the siphon to rapidly infuse marinades into meat and vegetables.

   - **Pro:** These siphons are incredibly versatile.
   - **Con:** The only downside is in the dispensing process. To get liquid out of these siphons, you need to turn the can upside down and press a button, as if you're dispensing whipped cream from a store-bought whipped cream can.

STAND-UP CARBONATION SYSTEMS

The Low-Down on Carbonation Systems:

- Carbonation systems use a large canister filled with carbon dioxide to fill reusable bottles.
- The best-known and most-established brands of at-home carbonators are Cuisinart and SodaStream.
- Stand-up carbonators range in price from $80 to more than $200. The more expensive models have features such as indicators that tell you how carbonated your water is, as well as extra charging cartridges and soda flavoring kits.

Most consumers are most familiar with stand-up carbonation systems. These systems feature a large canister filled with carbon dioxide and reusable bottles. To use these carbonators, you fill the bottle with plain water, attach the bottle to the carbonator, and press a button one or more times. The button releases carbon dioxide into the water. Once you remove the bottle from the system, you have a bottle of homemade club soda.

Stand-up carbonation systems require space on your kitchen countertop or home bar. Although they are fairly compact—the smallest one having a footprint of six inches by six inches—they are quite tall, and don't easily fit onto shelves or into drawers.

However, they are designed beautifully, and keeping one on your kitchen counter will not only encourage you to drink more carbonated water; it will add a sleek design element to your kitchen.

When you use a stand-up carbonator, you can carbonate only water (you'll add flavors in after you carbonate the water). Other fluids will leave debris, which can contaminate and/or clog your system.

BOTTLE-CAP CARBONATORS

The Low-Down on Bottle-Cap Carbonators

- These carbonators use a cap that holds a small carbon dioxide charger to carbonate water for a reusable 1-liter plastic bottle.
- This type of system is called Cuisinart Compact Sparkling Beverage Maker powered by SodaSparkle.

- The cartridges sold for bottle-cap carbonators are single-use only. You can buy the cartridges in bulk at housewares stores, and online.
- Bottle-cap carbonators have a price of $80.

The latest design for at-home carbonators is a bottle-cap system. These carbonators come with a reusable 1-liter plastic bottle and a cap that holds a small carbon dioxide charger. To use the system, you fill the bottle with water, add a cartridge to the charger cap, and twist the cap onto the bottle. The cap will release carbon dioxide into the water, and when you remove the cap, you have sparkling water.

Of the three types of carbonation systems, these devices are the smallest, most portable, and easiest to store. They are barely larger than a 1-liter bottle, and the cap can be stored in most utensil drawers. Although not unattractive, they are not designed to display on counters or bars.

When you use a bottle-cap carbonator, you can carbonate only water (you add in the flavors after you carbonate the water). Other fluids will leave debris, which can contaminate and/or clog your system.

Tips on Buying At-Home Carbonation Supplies

You can buy at-home carbonators in a variety of places. Here are some of the most common options:

- Online retailers, such as Amazon.com, have low prices and the widest variety of both carbonators and chargers. The only downside is that chargers must be shipped via ground transportation (because they are pressurized tanks), so you might have to wait up to a week before your order arrives.
- Mass retailers and department stores (Bloomingdale's, Macy's, Target, Walmart) also carry a wide variety of carbonators and chargers at very good prices. Plus, you can pick up the item right away and don't need to wait for it to be shipped.
- Kitchen stores, such as Bed Bath & Beyond, Sur La Table, and Williams-Sonoma, may carry fewer varieties of devices, but offer helpful sales clerks, who can expertly help you make decisions. They often carry the most stylish designs, so these are good places to find a carbonator if you'd like to display it in your kitchen or bar.

Buying the device is only one cost. Once you're making soda on a regular basis, you'll also spend money buying chargers and carbon dioxide tanks. If you have stand-up carbonator, it is most economical to take your tank to be refilled, rather than buying a whole new tank. Bed Bath & Beyond will refill tanks.

For small, nonrefillable chargers (used for siphons), sign up to receive e-newsletters from your carbonator's manufacturer as well as cookware stores. They will alert you to sales, and will sometimes offer discounts on their products. Alternately, you can look for coupons for retailers that carry chargers.

Other Equipment

Once you have chosen which at-home carbonation system to use, you'll need some additional kitchen equipment in order to flavor your sparkling water. The good news: the extra equipment needs are minimal, and are items that you probably have in your kitchen.

- You will always want to use **precise measuring cups and spoons**. Because small amounts of soda syrup are added to carbonated water, you'll want to ensure that you measure ingredients exactly to get the best results.

  - For measuring **liquids**, select heavy glass liquid measuring cups. Glass takes high heat better than plastic, and also stays clear and easy-to-read even after years of use and dishwashing. (Plastic often clouds when you wash it in the dishwasher.)
  - For **dry-ingredient** measuring cups and for measuring spoons, choose metal, as opposed to plastic. Metal will not shift and warp (like plastic can), meaning

your cups and spoons stay true to their measurements. Plastic can warp and crack, changing how much fits into the bowl of the cup or spoon and therefore affecting your measurements.

- When making cocktails and sparkling soft drinks, you'll also want to have a cache of **bar supplies**, such as muddlers, shakers, and strainers. You can find these at cookware stores, near glassware in department stores, or in liquor stores.

  - Many drinks will require you to smash fruit or fresh herbs. For this, invest in a **muddler**. This is a small, dense rod, about one inch in diameter and anywhere between six and eight inches long. It's usually made from metal or wood, and looks a little like a miniature baseball bat. The end may be rounded or may have small spikes. You use the end to crush soft fruit and fresh herbs into the bottom of a glass, thereby releasing the essential oils needed for flavoring a drink.
  - A **cocktail shaker** is also handy for in-home beverage making. It's a quick and easy container to use to blend ingredients and ice before straining into a glass and topping with a sparkling soft drink. Choose a shaker you can grip comfortably in one hand. The shaker should have a snug-fitting lid, so that you can shake your drink without liquid spilling out. Some shakers have a strainer top, meaning you can simply remove a small cap and strain your drink into a glass. Others require a separate strainer. For simplicity, and for compact storage, it's best to have a shaker with a strainer top. In terms of material, metal or plastic each have advantages. Metal chills the drink faster. However, plastic is lighter-weight (and easier to shake), plus stays a slightly warmer temperature, so you don't freeze your hand while shaking drinks.

- Many of the flavoring bases require cutting and/or peeling fruit. For this, you'll want a couple of **good knives**. You don't need many knives for making soda—a chef's knife and a paring knife will do—but you want to ensure they are high-quality. Purchase knives that feel comfortable in your grip, have blades that run the entire length of the knives' handles (which make for better-balanced and more durable knives), and have blades that can be sharpened. For best results, invest in a honing steel and hone your knives after every five to ten minutes of chopping. (This keeps your blade sharpest.) In addition, take your knives to be professionally sharpened once per year.
- **Peelers** are also handy for preparing fruits and vegetables. Ensure that the peeler feels comfortable in your grip. Make sure

the blade removes only a small amount of a fruit's or vegetable's peel. This is essential for peeling citrus, where the colored part has tasty essential oils, and the white part tastes very bitter. A peeler that removes too much peel will grab too much of the white part of citrus, imparting a bitter flavor to your drinks. Since peelers dull easily and are difficult to sharpen, you may want to consider inexpensive peelers that you replace every few years, or when they fail to peel easily.

- For finely grating citrus peel, you'll want a standard **grater or a microplane**. Look for a grater that has a side with small holes (usually used for grating hard cheeses). You could also consider a microplane, which is a tool that looks a bit like a rasp, but with small holes for grating hard cheeses and citrus. Which you select should depend on your other cooking needs, and how much storage space you have. If you would benefit from a tool that has several sizes of holes for different grating options (such as one for grating carrots or slicing cheese), select a box grater. If you mostly grate hard cheese, citrus peel, and chocolate, select a microplane. This flat tool stores easily in a utensil drawer, unlike a box grater, which takes up a lot of shelf space.

- Many of the syrup bases require a bit of cooking or simmering, for which you'll need a **saucepot**. Generally, the quantities are small, and will call for a 1-quart pot or smaller. Ensure you're using a nonreactive material—such as stainless steel or enamel-coated metal—because you'll be cooking fresh fruits, which have enzymes that can react with surfaces like cast iron and aluminum. Also make sure the handles are firmly attached, as you'll be pouring the contents of the pot into strainers, blenders, and funnels.

- A good **wire-mesh strainer** helps in home soda-making. Liquids that are too chunky are difficult to carbonate, and straining gets rid of the chunks by catching the peels, seeds, skins, and pulp that you want to keep out of your sodas. A good strainer has the mesh firmly attached to the hoop that holds it. Look for a strainer with a metal hoop, as opposed to a plastic hoop, as a metal hoop is more durable and won't warp when you strain hot liquids. Also find a strainer with a comfortable handle, as you will need to grip and shake the handle from time to time. You might also want a strainer with an additional loop or lip on the opposite end of the strainer from the handle to allow you to balance the strainer over a pot or bowl without you holding it.

- For highly refined syrups (those without pulp), you'll need **cheesecloth** for straining. You're welcome to decide whether bleached or unbleached cheesecloth suits you better. Both function the same. Unbleached cheesecloth looks a little darker, and is free from chemicals needed to bleach cheesecloth. However, bleached cheesecloth is usually easier to find. In fact, many grocery stores carry bleached cheesecloth (which, as the name implies, has been bleached with chlorine bleach to whiten it), whereas you may need to make a trip to a cookware store to find the unbleached variety. Either way, you are likely to be able to use the same piece of cheesecloth a few times. Once you are finished straining, simply rinse the cheesecloth well. Then wash it using hand dishwashing soap and warm water. Rinse thoroughly and air dry.

- Some fruits, such as berries or melons, will require **a blender or food processor** to turn the fruit into a soda base. If you already have a machine you like, there is no need to purchase a new one for soda-making. For the recipes in this book, you won't require an expensive machine with a high-horsepower engine. If you do need to buy one, make sure it has sharp blades, has a "pulse" mode (which is useful for blending hot mixtures, because it allows steam to escape), and is easy to clean.
- Finally, you'll need a **funnel** so that you can transfer syrup bases into storage containers. An inexpensive plastic funnel is just fine for this purpose. All recipes in this book have you completely cool liquids before you transfer them to storage containers or drinks, so you don't need a high-heat funnel. However, as with other

kitchen equipment, if you already have a funnel, use what you have on hand.

Now that you have your kitchen fully equipped for soda-making, it's time to learn about the process itself.

CHAPTER 3

Preparing Bases for Carbonation

Making your own flavoring to add to your fizzy water is where the real fun of at-home carbonation begins. You can make your own versions of commercially sold soda pops, such as colas and root beers, or you can make new flavors, such as fruits mixed with herbs, dry sodas, or even floral sodas! In order to flavor your sparkling water, you will first need to make a base.

What Is a Base?

A base is the flavor carrier for your soda, usually with the consistency of syrup, and will then be mixed with plain carbonated water to create a tasty beverage. Here are some simple tips for making bases:

- Make a base that will dissolve in water. Most water-based bases (like the recipes included in this book) and most powders dissolve in water. Oils, on the other hand, will not, and are therefore not good candidates for making syrup bases.
- Leave out foods with a lot of protein, such as milk, eggs, or soy beverages, which do not carbonate well. Instead, they create large bubbles on the surface of the beverage, rather than small bubbles within the beverage. (Think about the last time you blew into a glass of milk using a straw.)
- Choose any plant or food derived from plants for carbonated beverages. Fruits and vegetables carbonate well, as do spices, herbs, flowers, and sweeteners.
- Watch the consistency of your base. You don't want too many large particles in your drinks—carbonation can't penetrate solids. A quick strain through wire mesh or cheesecloth will ensure your base can take on carbonation.

How to Select Fruits, Vegetables, and Herbs for Bases

Selecting the best, most flavorful fruits, vegetables, and herbs will help make sure your final product tastes delicious. To ensure you're buying ingredients with the most flavor:

- Try to buy in-season ingredients. Farmers' markets or roadside stands are great spots to find in-season fruits, vegetables, and herbs.
- If you can't find in-season fruit, buy frozen options before you use a "fresh" option from the grocery store that's out of season and probably shipped from half a world away.
- If you can't find fresh herbs in season, go for dried. However, you'll want to use about ⅓ of the amount called for in the recipe. So if a recipe calls for 1 tablespoon fresh herbs, use ⅓ tablespoon (or 1 teaspoon) dried. Also make sure you use dried herbs that are less than a year old. After a year, dried herbs lose their volatile oils, which are what give them their distinct flavor.
- Select produce that is free from blemishes. Avoid brown spots, mold, and decay.
- Select produce that is dense and heavy for its relative size. Heavier fruits and veggies contain more juice, and are therefore the most flavorful.

Sweeteners

In this book, you will find recipes for regular beverages (like Ginger Ale and Lemon-Lime Soda), as well as for lower-calorie versions of some of these beverages (such as Low-Calorie Ginger Ale and Low-Calorie Lemon-Lime Soda). Both use sweeteners, but different types.

For the regular beverages, recipes call for white sugar, brown sugar, agave nectar, or honey to sweeten the base and give your soda a similar sugar level to store-bought beverages. These sweeteners are all-natural, are easily found, and carbonate well. If you prefer a less sweet beverage, feel free to experiment with the amount of sugar called for in the recipes. Adding or subtracting sugar will not materially affect your ability to carbonate the base.

Recipes for reduced-calorie beverages call for stevia powder. This all-natural, low-calorie sweetener is derived from the dried leaves of a South American herb. If you prefer to use a different sweetener, consult the sweetener's manufacturer for stevia equivalents and make a substitution in the low-calorie recipes.

There's No Substitute

Because sugar has different cooking properties than many low-calorie sweeteners, don't substitute a low-calorie sweetener in the recipes that call for sugar, honey, or agave.

Principles of Making Bases

You'll find a number of ways to make syrup bases contained in this cookbook:

- The most standard way is to make a simple syrup (one part granulated white sugar to one part water, boiled until clear) and steep a flavoring component (like fruit, zest, herbs, or spices) in the syrup until it cools. Then you strain the syrup and add it to carbonated water.
- For noncaloric sweeteners, the method is typically to make an unsweetened "stock" out of the flavors (fruit, herbs, spices), sweeten with stevia, then add to carbonation.
- In other cases, you'll purée fruits and strain them, then add the fruit base to carbonated water to make soda.

Regardless of how you make the base, the goal is to impart that syrup with lots of intense flavor that will then be dispersed throughout your drink or dish. Now, let's discuss how to take care of these bases after you make them.

CHAPTER 4

Storing Bases, Carbonating, and Post-Carbonation Care

Sometimes, you want to make a soda base well in advance of when you add the carbonated water to make soda. For example, if you're hosting a party, it's a good idea to make a lot of base so that you can quickly provide soft drinks at the time of the party. Or perhaps you find that your family goes through a particular type of soda quickly, and you'd benefit from making a double batch so you can always have your favorite drink on hand. Maybe you've found a great bargain on ingredients and you'd like to turn a large quantity of ingredients into soda base. This section explains the optimal ways of storing bases and how to tell when they are past their prime. It also gives you tips on making the perfect soda.

How to Store Your Bases

Regardless of the reason, if you have base to store, here are some techniques for safely storing bases:

- Use only *airtight* containers—you can choose among plastic resealable containers, plastic jars, plastic bottles, glass jars, or glass bottles. If your seal isn't airtight, or the container leaks, you let in air, which can create an environment for bacteria to grow. A loose seal also opens up the possibility that other foods in your fridge will change the flavor of your base (and no one likes garlic-flavored soda!).
- Make sure the base fills up as much of the container as possible. So if you make 2 cups of syrup, use a 2-cup container. This keeps out excess air, and therefore reduces the chances for bacteria.

> ### How to Test a Seal
> Not sure if the container you've selected for your base is airtight? There is an easy way to tell. Fill your container with plain tap water, put on the lid, and seal it. Then shake and invert the container over your sink. If any water comes out of the container, even a dribble, it's not airtight. Find a different container to use for your soda base.

- Always cool your bases to room temperature before storing, and then store them in a refrigerator that's between 34°F and 38°F. This process is essential for bases that have fresh or frozen fruit, and/or fresh herbs. Fresh produce will decay quickly when stored at room temperature—even though it's preserved with sugar syrup within the base. Refrigeration is also important for bases without fresh or frozen produce, though. Cool temps keep the volatile oils that flavor your bases from breaking down and changing flavor. Finally, chilled bases keep the level of carbonation steady. A warm or room-temperature base will deflate your soda.
- The shelf life for bases with fresh or frozen fruits and/or herbs is two weeks when stored in the refrigerator. The shelf life extends to three months if you freeze these bases. For other bases (such as the root beer or ginger ale bases), the shelf life is four weeks when refrigerated, or six months when frozen. If you freeze your bases, defrost them completely before adding to sparkling water.

> ### Keeping Track of Your Syrups
> You may find yourself with a growing collection of stored soda bases, but no recollection of what flavors they are, when they expire, or how much to mix into sparkling water. To solve this challenge, make sure you label each base with its name, the ratio of base to soda you use, and the date you made it. Then you can quickly grab your base, some soda, and whip up a tasty, sparkling beverage.

Achieving Perfect Carbonation

The key to making perfect sparkling beverages at home is to make the perfect club soda. In order to achieve perfection, follow a few simple tips:

1. Always follow the manufacturer's directions exactly. Your manufacturer built the carbonator, and therefore knows how to use it best. Don't try to improve on the manufacturer's results by trying new or different directions.

2. Always use accessories that are made or approved by your device's manufacturer. You may be tempted to save money by buying a less expensive CO2 charger, or retrofitting a bottle to fit your carbonator. However, each manufacturer makes bottles, dispensers, chargers, and accessories that fit exactly into its devices. Accessories—especially chargers—made by other manufacturers will not fit perfectly, and you run the risk of adding too much or too little carbonation into your water. In some cases, you may even cause the bottle to shoot off the carbonator. In addition, you will void manufacturers' warranties by using noncertified parts. What may appear to save you a few dollars could cost you hundreds if you have to buy a whole new machine.

3. Chill water before carbonating it. Cold water holds carbonation much better than warm or room-temperature water. For optimal results, make sure you chill water in your refrigerator for four hours prior to carbonating it.

4. Add a pinch or two of fine salt to a liter or quart of chilled water before you carbonate it. The solid salt particles will help the bubbles to form. Be sure to use fine salt! Coarse salt, such as flaked sea salt or large grains of kosher salt, doesn't have the same effect. If you only have large grains of salt available, crush them with a mortar and pestle or grind them in a food processor, blender, or spice grinder.

Other Uses for Syrups and Bases

If you have lots of leftover soda bases and you're worried about using them while they're still fresh, put your mind at ease. In addition to making sparkling beverages, syrups are great in other beverages, such as black or green tea, or to flavor milkshakes or smoothies. They're also a terrific topping on thick, Greek yogurt, frozen yogurt, or ice cream. Or, for a sweet-savory delight, fruit bases make tasty glazes for poultry or pork. You may even want to stir in some fresh herbs or a teaspoon of Dijon mustard to add more complex flavor.

Adding a Base to Carbonated Water

When you're ready to flavor your water, there are a few tricks that help the base mix with the soda water and keep optimal carbonation:

- **Make sure the water and the base are both chilled.** Water holds carbonation best at temperatures close to freezing. Be sure to chill your water before you carbonate it, carbonate it right away, and then keep it on ice or in the refrigerator until you're ready to mix in the base. It's also essential that the base is completely chilled before you add it to your carbonated water, as a warm base will increase the temperature of the drink and therefore reduce the amount of carbonation in it. For best results, make your bases a day before you want to drink them, and keep the prepared bases in your refrigerator until you're ready to mix them into soda water.

- **Pour a small amount of carbonated water into a glass and check if it's carbonated to your liking.** If the water is undercarbonated, follow the manufacturer's instructions for adding more carbonation. If the water is overcarbonated, cap the bottle tightly and *gently* rock the bottle back and forth; then uncap and test carbonation levels. A gentle agitation will energize the carbonation within the water, making it release carbonation quickly once the bottle is uncapped.

- **Flavor soda in small quantities that you're guaranteed to consume in a single sitting.** Even under the best circumstances, carbonated beverages lose their fizz. By making only what you'll drink at one time, you can avoid flat soda.

- **Measure the base and carbonated water accurately.** For a recipe to taste right, you'll need to have the correct ratio of water to base. Estimating the amount of base to use for a drink will result in soda that is either too concentrated, or not strong enough.

- **Mix very gently.** Gentle stirring or swirling will mix the carbonated water with the base without releasing too much carbonation. Shaking or vigorous stirring, on the other hand, will cause a quick release of carbon dioxide from the water, resulting in a drink that bubbles over and goes flat quickly.

- **Mix the base and carbonated water in a glass or cup, rather than in the soda bottle.** To properly carbonate a bottle of water, that bottle must be nearly filled. (Manufacturers provide fill lines on their bottles, so you will know the right amount.) For many of the recipes in this book, the syrup needed to flavor a whole bottle of water will not fit within the bottle along with all the water. In addition, if you add a base to your bottle, you will need to clean that bottle thoroughly before you use it again. Most of the bottles that work with in-home carbonators are hand-wash only. While it's not difficult to hand wash bottles, it is time-consuming. And, finally, by mixing the water and base outside the bottle, you're more likely to use moderation when mixing. It's too great a temptation to shake a bottle enthusiastically when combining the base and water within the bottle.

Is It Still Good?

If you've forgotten to label your base and are not sure if it's still good, there are a few ways to test for freshness. First, open the container and give it a sniff. The base should smell like it did when you initially made it. If it doesn't, throw it out. If the top of the syrup is oily or foamy, throw it out. Also, any syrup that you've strained (such as cola syrup or ginger ale syrup) should still be clear. Cloudy syrup indicates decay. Some soda bases will separate. That's ok—just give them a quick shake or stir before you add them to carbonated water.

Recarbonating

You may find that your soda water or carbonated beverages lose their fizz or go "flat" over time. When this happens, you may wonder how to add fizz back into your drinks.

PLAIN WATER

It is perfectly safe to recarbonate plain water or water with a pinch of salt. If you have a bottle of plain soda water that isn't quite as bubbly as you'd like, simply carbonate it again, using the manufacturer's directions.

FLAVORED WATERS

If you have already flavored your water, it's not so simple. At-home carbonators are made to add bubbles to plain water only, or water with just a trace of salt. If you carbonate anything other than water, food particles transfer to the machine and to the carbonation source. These will decay in time, and create an environment that's ripe for bacteria. Once your carbonator is infected with bacteria, it can transport bacteria to everything it touches, including new bottles of water you're carbonating. However, if you have a siphon that is made for whipped cream and other foods, you can use that siphon to recarbonate flat sodas. Place the flat soda into the siphon, and follow the manufacturer's directions for carbonating drinks.

So what do you do when your fizzy flavored drink is not-so-fizzy?

1. **For small quantities of drinks**, like less than 2 cups, you can mix in more soda water. Start by carbonating some plain water to a really high level of carbonation, past the point where you would prefer to drink it. Add a little of this overcarbonated water to your sparkling drink, a tablespoon at a time. You may be able to add enough bubbles to your drink without diluting the flavor too much. If you're able to achieve the right level of carbonation, but the drink tastes watered down, add flavoring base to the drink ½ teaspoon at a time to correct the taste.

2. **For flavored drinks that are more than 2 cups**, there is no effective way to recarbonate. Instead, use this drink as a brine, in a marinade, or in a sauce, where the flavor is key but the carbonation itself isn't as important.

Part 2

RECIPES FOR CARBONATION BASES

Now that you've mastered the ins and outs of basic carbonation, it's time to delve into adding delicious flavors to your soda water. From basic to unique, you'll find something the whole family will enjoy in the following chapters. All you need is a quick trip to your garden, farmers' market, or local grocer and a little time in your kitchen.

CHAPTER 5

Classic Sodas

Whether you're a fan of cola, root beer, ginger ale—or the diet version of any of these—you can make a drink that replicates your favorite store version. Making classic sodas is a great place to start because you are familiar with the tastes and smells already, so you know how the drink "should" taste. The benefits of at-home carbonation are still plentiful, however—you can tweak the traditional flavors a bit here and there to make them even more to your liking!

Cola

Cola is truly a global drink. Initially popular in the United States in the nineteenth century, cola is now found on every continent. And it's no wonder! Cola contains universally popular flavors of citrus, coffee, and vanilla. The cola recipe here is not an exact taste replica of any cola in the marketplace, but you will recognize it as cola instantly. It's also a little lighter in color, resembling ginger ale in appearance.

MAKES 1 CUP SYRUP, ENOUGH TO FLAVOR 1 QUART OR 1 LITER CARBONATED WATER

1 quart plus 1 cup chilled water, divided

1 cup white sugar

1 teaspoon dark brown sugar

Zest of 1 orange, grated

Zest of 1 lemon, grated

Zest of 1 lime, grated

Pinch ground cinnamon

Pinch ground nutmeg

Pinch ground fennel, or 3–4 whole fennel seeds

¼ teaspoon ground dried ginger

2 teaspoons vanilla extract

2 teaspoons brewed strong coffee, chilled

1 (8" × 16") piece cheesecloth

1. Carbonate 1 quart water with your soda maker, following the manufacturer's directions. Chill on ice or in the refrigerator until cold, about 20 minutes on ice or 1 hour in the fridge.

2. Place white sugar, brown sugar, orange zest, lemon zest, lime zest, cinnamon, nutmeg, fennel, and ginger into the bowl of a blender or food processor. Pulse 3–4 times to mix well.

3. Then run continuously on high to grind into a fine powder, about 5 minutes. Transfer to a 1-quart heavy saucepan.

4. Add 1 cup water to pan. Bring to a boil over medium heat. Then simmer, uncovered, for 20 minutes.

5. Remove syrup from heat and allow to cool to room temperature, stirring occasionally, about 1 hour. Add vanilla and coffee.

6. Rinse cheesecloth under cold water. Wring out and fold in half so that you have a square. Line a funnel with cheesecloth. Pour syrup into a storage container through the cheesecloth-lined funnel. Refrigerate until cold, about 4 hours.

7. To make cola, add 1 cup syrup to each quart of chilled carbonated water. Stir well.

Low-Calorie Cola

With a popularity that rivals—and eclipses in some circles—that of regular cola, diet cola is a grocery-store mainstay. Unlike most diet colas made by manufacturers, this recipe uses stevia, an all-natural, organic sweetener. Colas you purchase generally use artificial sweeteners, such as aspartame (NutraSweet), saccharine, or sucralose (Splenda). Remember, at-home carbonation means that you can reap the benefits of controlling the ingredients you're using!

MAKES 1 CUP SYRUP, ENOUGH TO FLAVOR 1 QUART OR 1 LITER CARBONATED WATER

1 quart plus 1 cup chilled water, divided

Zest of 1 orange, finely grated

Zest of 1 lemon, finely grated

Zest of 1 lime, finely grated

Pinch ground cinnamon

Pinch ground nutmeg

Pinch ground fennel, or 5–6 whole fennel seeds

¼ teaspoon ground dried ginger

⅓ cup stevia

¼ teaspoon molasses

½ teaspoon vanilla extract

2 teaspoons brewed strong coffee, chilled

1 (8" × 16") piece cheesecloth

1. Carbonate 1 quart water with your soda maker, following the manufacturer's directions. Chill on ice or in the refrigerator until cold, about 20 minutes on ice or 1 hour in the fridge.

2. Place remaining water, orange zest, lemon zest, lime zest, cinnamon, nutmeg, fennel, and ginger into a 1-quart heavy saucepan. Bring to a boil over medium heat. Then simmer, uncovered, for 20 minutes.

3. Remove mixture from heat, stir in stevia, and allow to cool to room temperature, stirring occasionally, about 1 hour.

4. Rinse cheesecloth under cold water. Wring out and fold in half so that you have a square. Line a funnel with cheesecloth. Pour syrup into a storage container through the cheesecloth-lined funnel. Add molasses, vanilla, and coffee. Stir to combine. Refrigerate until cold, about 4 hours.

5. To make cola, add 1 cup syrup to each quart of chilled carbonated water. Stir well.

Lemon-Lime Soda

Lemon-lime soda goes by different names at the grocery store: Sprite, 7UP, or Sierra Mist. Whatever brand you prefer, it's a delicious combination of sweet and tart—but many store brands contain excessive sweeteners and artificial ingredients. Luckily, you can make your own lemon-lime soda at home with just a handful of natural ingredients. In addition, making your own at home means you can control the sugar. Use this recipe as a starting point for lemon-lime soda, and adjust the sugar to your liking in future batches.

MAKES 1 CUP SYRUP, ENOUGH TO FLAVOR 1 QUART OR 1 LITER CARBONATED WATER

1 quart plus ½ cup chilled water, divided

1½ lemons

3 limes

½ cup sugar

⅛ teaspoon salt, preferably a natural salt like kosher or sea salt

Pinch dried rosemary

1. Carbonate 1 quart water with your soda maker, following the manufacturer's directions. Chill on ice or in the refrigerator until cold, about 20 minutes on ice or 1 hour in the fridge.

2. Using a peeler, remove the zests from the lemons and the limes, ensuring you remove only the colored part and leave the white behind. Place zests into a small saucepot.

3. Juice lemons and limes together into a storage container, straining out seeds. Store in refrigerator.

4. Add sugar, remaining water, salt, and rosemary to the saucepot with zests. Bring to a boil over medium heat. Remove from heat and allow to cool to room temperature, about 30 minutes.

5. Strain out zests and rosemary and stir in reserved citrus juices. Transfer to a storage container and refrigerate until cold, about 4 hours.

6. To make soda, place ¼ cup syrup into a glass. Add 1 cup chilled carbonated water and stir gently. Add ice, if desired, and serve.

Low-Calorie Lemon-Lime Soda

Fresh lemons and limes make terrific low-calorie additions to carbonated water because they're packed with intense flavor. This recipe, made with fresh citrus and stevia, mimics the regular lemon-lime soda—it has a full, sweet flavor, but not a lot of calories!

MAKES 1 CUP SYRUP, ENOUGH TO FLAVOR 1 QUART OR 1 LITER CARBONATED WATER

1 quart plus ½ cup chilled water, divided

1½ lemons

3 limes

⅛ teaspoon salt, preferably a natural salt like kosher or sea salt

Pinch dried rosemary

¼ cup stevia

1. Carbonate 1 quart water with your soda maker, following the manufacturer's directions. Chill on ice or in the refrigerator until cold, about 20 minutes on ice or 1 hour in the fridge.

2. Using a peeler, remove the zests from the lemons and the limes, ensuring you remove only the colored part and leave the white behind. Place zests into a small saucepot.

3. Juice lemons and limes together into a storage container, straining out seeds. Store in refrigerator.

4. Add remaining water, salt, and rosemary to the saucepot with zests. Bring to a boil over medium heat. Remove from heat, stir in stevia, and allow to cool to room temperature, about 30 minutes.

5. Strain out zests and rosemary and stir reserved citrus juices. Transfer to a storage container and refrigerate until cold, about 4 hours.

6. To make soda, place ¼ cup syrup into a glass. Add 1 cup chilled carbonated water and stir gently. Add ice, if desired, and serve.

Root Beer

Root beer is traditionally a lightly alcoholic drink brewed from the roots of sapling trees. The primary root used in flavoring root beer was sassafras, but it is no longer sold in the United States due to health concerns. (Dried sassafras leaves, also known as filé or gumbo filé, are safe and still sold legally.) However, you can make a tasty root beer at home, even without sassafras roots. This combination of ginger root, herbs, spices, and vanilla makes for a robust root beer.

MAKES 1 CUP SYRUP, ENOUGH TO FLAVOR 1 QUART OR 1 LITER CARBONATED WATER

1 quart plus 1 cup chilled water, divided

1 vanilla bean

1 (6") licorice root, or ¼ cup licorice root pieces

1 (1") piece fresh ginger, peeled and cut into ½" disks

2 cloves

1 whole star anise pod

4 allspice berries

1 (4") cinnamon stick

1 cup light brown sugar

1 tablespoon molasses

¼–½ teaspoon wintergreen extract

1. Carbonate 1 quart water with your soda maker, following the manufacturer's directions. Chill on ice or in the refrigerator until cold, about 20 minutes on ice or 1 hour in the fridge.

2. Place remaining water into a heavy medium saucepan. Split vanilla bean lengthwise. Scrape seeds into saucepan with water.

3. Add scraped vanilla pod, licorice root, ginger, cloves, star anise, allspice, cinnamon stick, and brown sugar. Bring to a boil over medium heat. Remove from heat and cover. Let steep 1 hour.

4. Strain mixture into a storage container and stir in molasses and ¼ teaspoon of wintergreen extract. Refrigerate until completely cold, about 4 hours.

5. To make root beer, place ¼ cup root beer syrup into a glass. Top with 1 cup sparkling water. Stir gently. Add ice, if desired, and serve.

Adding More Kick

If, after tasting the first glass of root beer, you would like a bit more "kick," add a few drops (up to the remaining ¼ teaspoon) of wintergreen extract to the rest of the syrup. Wintergreen extract is very strong, so a little will change the flavor of your root beer syrup dramatically.

Low-Calorie Root Beer

Bursting with spices and complex flavors, root beer is a great candidate for making into a reduced-calorie soda. The spices work well with sweeteners that taste sweet—but decidedly different—from sugar, and can camouflage any "diet" taste.

MAKES 1 CUP SYRUP, ENOUGH TO FLAVOR 1 QUART OR 1 LITER CARBONATED WATER

1 quart plus 1 cup chilled water, divided

1 vanilla bean

1 (6") licorice root, or ¼ cup licorice root pieces

1 (1") piece fresh ginger, peeled and cut into ½" disks

2 cloves

1 whole star anise pod

4 allspice berries

1 (4") cinnamon stick

⅓ cup stevia

1 tablespoon molasses

¼–½ teaspoon wintergreen extract

1. Carbonate 1 quart water with your soda maker, following the manufacturer's directions. Chill on ice or in the refrigerator until cold, about 20 minutes on ice or 1 hour in the fridge.

2. Place remaining water into a heavy medium saucepan. Split vanilla bean lengthwise. Scrape seeds into saucepan with water.

3. Add scraped vanilla pod, licorice root, ginger, cloves, star anise, allspice, and cinnamon stick. Bring to a boil over medium heat. Remove from heat, stir in stevia, and cover. Let steep 1 hour.

4. Strain mixture into a storage container and stir in molasses and ¼ teaspoon of wintergreen extract. Refrigerate until completely cold, about 4 hours.

5. To make root beer, place ¼ cup root beer syrup into a glass. Top with 1 cup sparkling water. Stir gently. Add ice, if desired, and serve.

Ginger Ale

If you like spicy, piquant store-bought ginger ale, you will love this homemade soda even more. Bursting with the complex flavor that comes from both fresh and dried ginger, and accented with spices and honey, this ginger ale is a real treat. It's great whether you drink it on its own, in an ice-cream float, or paired with your favorite whiskey in a cocktail.

MAKES 1 CUP SYRUP, ENOUGH TO FLAVOR 1 QUART OR 1 LITER CARBONATED WATER

1 quart plus 1 cup chilled water, divided

1 (6") piece fresh ginger, peeled and cut into ¼" disks

¾ cup white sugar

¼ cup honey

Zest of 1 lemon, removed in large pieces with a vegetable peeler

1 teaspoon whole black peppercorns

Pinch ground cinnamon

¼ teaspoon ground dried ginger

¼ teaspoon vanilla extract

1. Carbonate 1 quart water with your soda maker, following the manufacturer's directions. Chill on ice or in the refrigerator until cold, about 20 minutes on ice or 1 hour in the fridge.

2. Place fresh ginger, sugar, honey, lemon zest, and peppercorns into a small saucepan with remaining water. Bring to a boil over medium heat. Then simmer, uncovered, for 20 minutes.

3. Remove syrup from heat and stir in cinnamon and dried ginger. Allow to cool to room temperature, stirring occasionally, about 1 hour. Add vanilla.

4. Using a slotted spoon, remove fresh ginger and peppercorns from syrup. Pour syrup into a storage container.

5. To make ginger ale, add ¼ cup syrup to a glass. Add 1 cup chilled carbonated water. Stir gently. Add ice, if desired, and serve.

Judging Syrups

You may be tempted to evaluate a syrup base on its own, before adding sparkling water. Be warned that this type of tasting isn't the optimal way to test whether the soda is to your liking. Carbonation will amplify some flavors while muting others, and change some altogether, meaning that your base will taste vastly different once you add it to sparkling water. For this reason, it's best to taste these sodas with the water. Make each base according to the recipe and completely chill it. Then add the recommended amount of chilled soda water to the base and stir gently. Now it's ready to taste.

Low-Calorie Ginger Ale

This low-calorie ginger ale has the same bite as regular homemade ginger ale, but with half the calories. A combination of sweeteners—honey and stevia—brings out the flavor of the fresh and dried ginger in this brew. If you would like to reduce the calories even further, omit the honey and double the amount of stevia used.

MAKES 1 CUP SYRUP, ENOUGH TO FLAVOR 1 QUART OR 1 LITER CARBONATED WATER

1 quart plus 1 cup chilled water, divided

1 (6") piece fresh ginger, peeled and cut into ¼" disks

¼ cup honey

Zest of 1 lemon, removed in large pieces with a vegetable peeler

1 teaspoon whole black peppercorns

¼ cup stevia

Pinch ground cinnamon

¼ teaspoon ground dried ginger

¼ teaspoon vanilla extract

1. Carbonate 1 quart water with your soda maker, following the manufacturer's directions. Chill on ice or in the refrigerator until cold, about 20 minutes on ice or 1 hour in the fridge.

2. Place fresh ginger, honey, lemon zest, and peppercorns into a small saucepan with remaining water. Bring to a boil over medium heat. Then simmer, uncovered, for 20 minutes.

3. Remove syrup from heat and stir in stevia, cinnamon, and dried ginger. Allow to cool to room temperature, stirring occasionally, about 1 hour. Add vanilla.

4. Using a slotted spoon, remove fresh ginger and peppercorns from syrup. Pour syrup into a storage container. Refrigerate until cold, about 4 hours.

5. To make ginger ale, add ¼ cup syrup to a glass. Add 1 cup chilled carbonated water. Stir gently. Add ice, if desired, and serve.

Vanilla Cream Soda

Vanilla cream soda is a luscious combination of crisp, bright bubbles; warm spice; and a delightful mouthfeel. To make the best vanilla cream soda, invest in whole vanilla beans, rather than using vanilla extract. The beans will impart a sweeter flavor, without any of the aftertaste that you sometimes get from extract or vanilla flavoring. After making the syrup, store the vanilla pods in plain sugar to make vanilla-scented sugar, which is terrific in baked goods.

MAKES 1 CUP SYRUP, ENOUGH TO FLAVOR 1 LITER OR 1 QUART CARBONATED WATER

1 quart plus 1 cup chilled water, divided

1 cup sugar

1 vanilla bean

¼ teaspoon ground nutmeg

¼ teaspoon almond extract

¼ cup heavy whipping cream

1. Carbonate 1 quart water with your soda maker, following the manufacturer's directions. Chill on ice or in the refrigerator until cold, about 20 minutes on ice or 1 hour in the fridge.

2. Place remaining water and sugar into a small saucepot. Using a paring knife, split vanilla bean in half lengthwise. Using the tip of your knife, scrape seeds from each pod half into pot. Add scraped pod halves and nutmeg. Bring to a boil over medium-high heat.

3. Remove from heat and let syrup cool to room temperature, about 1 hour. Remove pod halves and transfer syrup to a storage container. Stir in almond extract and cream and chill until very cold, about 4 hours.

4. To make soda, place ¼ cup syrup into a tall glass and top with 1 cup of sparkling water. Stir gently and serve.

Carbonating Dairy

In the first sections of this book, you read that dairy and other high-protein and high-fat beverages don't carbonate well. However, this recipe and other "cream" recipes call for dairy products. The small amount of cream or dairy in these recipes will not materially affect the fizz in your drinks. A mere ¼ cup goes into 1 liter of soda, which still leaves the majority of the drink easy to carbonate. However, if you find that the cream flattens your soda, simply start with sparkling water that is more carbonated than you typically prefer.

Low-Calorie Vanilla Cream Soda

A low-calorie indulgence that feels like a drink and dessert at the same time, this vanilla soda really satisfies. To draw as much vanilla flavor out of the vanilla beans as possible, this recipe makes it in a "sugary" simple syrup. However, you omit the need for sugar by bringing the cream to a boil with the vanilla pod. Using cream will extract as much vanilla flavor as sugar does, enabling you to use a noncaloric sweetener instead of sugar.

MAKES 1 CUP SYRUP, ENOUGH TO FLAVOR 1 LITER OR 1 QUART CARBONATED WATER

1 quart plus 1 cup chilled water, divided

1 vanilla bean

¼ cup heavy whipping cream

¼ teaspoon ground nutmeg

¼ cup stevia

¼ teaspoon almond extract

1. Carbonate 1 quart water with your soda maker, following the manufacturer's directions. Chill on ice or in the refrigerator until cold, about 20 minutes on ice or 1 hour in the fridge.

2. Place remaining water into a small saucepot. Using a paring knife, split vanilla bean in half lengthwise. Using the tip of your knife, scrape seeds from each pod half into pot. Add scraped pod halves, cream, and nutmeg. Bring to a boil over medium-high heat.

3. Remove from heat, stir in stevia, and let mixture cool to room temperature, about an hour. Remove pod halves and transfer liquid to a storage container. Stir in almond extract, and chill until very cold, about 4 hours.

4. To make soda, place ¼ cup syrup into a tall glass and top with 1 cup of sparkling water. Stir gently and serve.

Orange Cream Soda

Like an effervescent dreamsicle, orange cream soda blends the slightly tart flavor of orange with rich cream. Because the base for this soda contains dairy, which doesn't carbonate well, you'll want to slightly overcarbonate the soda water you mix into the base. This way, the milk fat and proteins contained in the half and half won't leave you with flat soda.

MAKES 1⅓ CUPS SYRUP, ENOUGH TO FLAVOR 1 QUART OR 1 LITER CARBONATED WATER

1 quart chilled water

2 oranges (any variety with a thick skin, such as navel, Cara Cara, or blood orange)

½ cup half and half

Pinch ground nutmeg

Pinch ground allspice

½ cup sugar

½ teaspoon vanilla extract

1. Carbonate 1 quart water with your soda maker, following the manufacturer's directions. Chill on ice or in the refrigerator until cold, about 20 minutes on ice or 1 hour in the fridge.

2. Remove zest from oranges in long, thin strips. Juice oranges, straining out seeds, and reserve juice in a container in the refrigerator.

3. Place zest, half and half, nutmeg, allspice, and sugar into a small saucepot. Bring to a boil over medium heat and immediately remove from heat.

4. Cover pot and let stand 20 minutes. Remove zest using tongs or a slotted spoon. Cool mixture to room temperature, about 1 hour. Stir in vanilla and reserved orange juice. Chill in the refrigerator until completely cold, at least 4 hours.

5. To make soda, stir ⅓ cup of base into 1 cup of sparkling water.

Low-Calorie Orange Cream Soda

Relying on the natural sweetness of oranges, and the lush flavor of half and half, this decadent cream soda barely needs sweeteners. The regular-calorie version requires ½ cup of sugar, while this reduced-calorie version needs only 2 tablespoons of stevia.

MAKES 1⅓ CUPS SYRUP, ENOUGH TO FLAVOR 1 QUART OR 1 LITER CARBONATED WATER

1 quart chilled water

2 oranges (any variety with a thick skin, such as navel, Cara Cara, or blood orange)

½ cup half and half

Pinch ground nutmeg

Pinch ground allspice

2 tablespoons stevia

½ teaspoon vanilla extract

1. Carbonate 1 quart water with your soda maker, following the manufacturer's directions. Chill on ice or in the refrigerator until cold, about 20 minutes on ice or 1 hour in the fridge.

2. Remove zest from oranges in long, thin strips. Juice oranges, straining out seeds, and reserve juice in a container in the refrigerator.

3. Place zest, half and half, nutmeg, and allspice into a small saucepot. Bring to a boil over medium heat and immediately remove from heat.

4. Cover pot and let stand 20 minutes. Remove zest using tongs or a slotted spoon and stir in stevia. Cool mixture to room temperature, about 1 hour. Stir in vanilla and reserved orange juice. Chill in the refrigerator until completely cold, at least 4 hours.

5. To make soda, stir ⅓ cup of base into 1 cup of sparkling water.

Substituting Other Reduced-Calorie Sweeteners

This book uses stevia as a low-calorie sweetener. If you'd like to use a sweetener other than stevia, follow the lower-calorie versions of the recipes in this book, omit the stevia, and add your sweetener of choice to taste when you mix the soda base with carbonated water.

Vanilla Cola

This cola takes the flavors of traditional cola up a notch with the addition of vanilla. For this reason, you'll want to use a vanilla bean, in addition to vanilla extract. Adding a bit of almond extract at the end further amplifies the vanilla taste.

MAKES 1 CUP SYRUP, ENOUGH TO FLAVOR 1 QUART OR 1 LITER CARBONATED WATER

1 quart plus 1 cup chilled water, divided

2 vanilla beans

1 cup white sugar

1 teaspoon dark brown sugar

Zest of 1 orange, grated

Zest of 1 lemon, grated

Zest of 1 lime, grated

Pinch ground cinnamon

Pinch ground nutmeg

Pinch ground fennel, or 3–4 whole fennel seeds

¼ teaspoon ground dried ginger

2 teaspoons vanilla extract

¼ teaspoon almond extract

2 teaspoons brewed strong coffee, chilled

1 (8" × 16") piece cheesecloth

1. Carbonate 1 quart water with your soda maker, following the manufacturer's directions. Chill on ice or in the refrigerator until cold, about 20 minutes on ice or 1 hour in the fridge.

2. Split vanilla beans lengthwise. Scrape seeds into the bowl of a blender or food processor and set aside. Place scraped vanilla pods into a 1-quart heavy saucepot.

3. Add white sugar, brown sugar, orange zest, lemon zest, lime zest, cinnamon, nutmeg, fennel, and ginger into the blender or food processor that has the vanilla seeds. Pulse 3–4 times to mix well. Then run continuously on high to grind into a fine powder, about 5 minutes. Transfer to saucepot along with vanilla pods.

4. Add 1 cup water to pot. Bring to a boil over medium heat. Then simmer, uncovered, for 20 minutes.

5. Remove syrup from heat and allow to cool to room temperature, stirring occasionally, about 1 hour. Add vanilla extract, almond extract, and coffee.

6. Rinse cheesecloth under cold water. Wring out and fold in half so that you have a square. Line a funnel with cheesecloth. Pour syrup into a storage container through the cheesecloth-lined funnel. Refrigerate until cold, about 4 hours.

7. To make vanilla cola, place ¼ cup syrup into a cup. Add 1 cup chilled carbonated water. Stir gently. Add ice, if desired, and serve.

Adding Vanilla to a Cola Base

This recipe makes vanilla cola from scratch, but if you have cola base on hand, you can flavor it without making a whole new batch of syrup. Simply bring ¼ cup white sugar plus ¼ cup water to a boil. (You can even do it in the microwave.) Swirl and let sit until the syrup is clear. Add 1 teaspoon vanilla extract plus 2–3 drops almond extract. Let mixture cool completely. Make a glass of Cola using the recipe in this chapter. Add the vanilla syrup to taste and enjoy!

Low-Calorie Vanilla Cola

The extra vanilla bean in this recipe allows the vanilla flavoring to shine through, so you don't even miss the white sugar. Because stevia has vanilla notes in its flavor profile, you're able to use slightly less vanilla than in the regular vanilla cola recipe.

MAKES 1 CUP SYRUP, ENOUGH TO FLAVOR 1 QUART OR 1 LITER CARBONATED WATER

1 quart plus 1 cup chilled water, divided

2 vanilla beans

Zest of 1 orange, finely grated

Zest of 1 lemon, finely grated

Zest of 1 lime, finely grated

Pinch ground cinnamon

Pinch ground nutmeg

Pinch ground fennel, or 5–6 whole fennel seeds

¼ teaspoon ground dried ginger

⅓ cup stevia

1 (8" × 16") piece cheesecloth

¼ teaspoon molasses

½ teaspoon vanilla extract

¼ teaspoon almond extract

2 teaspoons brewed strong coffee, chilled

1. Carbonate 1 quart water with your soda maker, following the manufacturer's directions. Chill on ice or in the refrigerator until cold, about 20 minutes on ice or 1 hour in the fridge.

2. Split vanilla beans lengthwise. Scrape seeds into a 1-quart heavy saucepot. Add vanilla pods, remaining water, orange zest, lemon zest, lime zest, cinnamon, nutmeg, fennel, and ginger.

3. Bring to a boil over medium heat. Then simmer, uncovered, for 20 minutes.

4. Remove mixture from heat, stir in stevia, and allow to cool to room temperature, stirring occasionally, about 1 hour.

5. Rinse cheesecloth under cold water. Wring out and fold in half so that you have a square. Line a funnel with cheesecloth. Pour syrup into a storage container through the cheesecloth-lined funnel. Add molasses, vanilla extract, almond extract, and coffee. Stir to combine. Refrigerate until cold, about 4 hours.

6. To make vanilla cola, place ¼ cup syrup into a cup. Add 1 cup chilled carbonated water. Stir gently. Add ice, if desired, and serve.

Cherry Cola

Rich, citrus-spicy cola comes to life with the addition of summer-ripe cherries. Commercial manufacturers use the flavor of sweet cherries to flavor their colas, but try experimenting at home! Make this recipe with sweet cherries one time, sour the next, or even a combination of the two.

MAKES 1 CUP SYRUP, ENOUGH TO FLAVOR 1 QUART OR 1 LITER CARBONATED WATER

1 quart plus 1 cup chilled water, divided

1 cup white sugar

1 teaspoon dark brown sugar

Zest of 1 orange, grated

Zest of 1 lemon, grated

Zest of 1 lime, grated

Pinch ground cinnamon

Pinch ground nutmeg

Pinch ground fennel, or 3–4 whole fennel seeds

¼ teaspoon ground dried ginger

½ cup cherries, stemmed, but not pitted

1 (8" × 16") piece cheesecloth

1 teaspoon vanilla extract

¼ teaspoon almond extract

2 teaspoons brewed strong coffee, chilled

¼ teaspoon citric acid

1. Carbonate 1 quart water with your soda maker, following the manufacturer's directions. Chill on ice or in the refrigerator until cold, about 20 minutes on ice or 1 hour in the fridge.

2. Place white sugar, brown sugar, orange zest, lemon zest, lime zest, cinnamon, nutmeg, fennel, and ginger into the bowl of a blender or food processor. Pulse 3–4 times to mix well. Then run continuously on high to grind into a fine powder, about 5 minutes. Transfer to a 1-quart heavy saucepan.

3. Add remaining water and cherries to pan. Bring to a boil over medium heat. Then simmer, uncovered, for 20 minutes.

4. Remove syrup from heat and allow to cool to room temperature, stirring occasionally, about 1 hour. Strain through a wire-mesh sieve, pressing on solids with the back of a wooden spoon to extract as much liquid as possible.

5. If you are happy with how clear the liquid is, skip to the next step. Otherwise, strain a second time: Rinse cheesecloth under cold water. Wring out and fold in half so that you have a square. Line a funnel with cheesecloth. Pour syrup into a storage container through the cheesecloth-lined funnel.

6. Add vanilla extract, almond extract, coffee, and citric acid. Refrigerate mixture until well chilled, about 4 hours.

7. To make cherry cola, place ¼ cup syrup into the bottom of a glass. Add 1 cup chilled carbonated water. Stir gently. Add ice, if desired, and serve.

Why Citric Acid?

When making natural sodas at home, it's reasonable to question why recipes call for citric acid and whether you should use it. After all, one of the reasons you're making soda in the first place may be to cut extraneous chemicals and ingredients out of your diet. Citric acid, with an ominous-sounding name, is actually natural and quite safe. It is made from dried, crystallized citrus juice (most commonly lemons and limes). Citric acid adds a hint of sourness to food and drinks, and is especially welcome in citrus sodas, where it enhances the flavor of the fruit. Citric acid is also a natural preservative, and will prolong the life of your soda syrups. If you have problems finding citric acid, you may substitute 2 teaspoons of distilled white vinegar (unflavored) for each ¼ teaspoon of citric acid.

Low-Calorie Cherry Cola

Decadent cherry cola is terrific with stevia, too. You'll get the same delicious flavor without the guilt of unnecessary calories.

MAKES 1 CUP SYRUP, ENOUGH TO FLAVOR 1 QUART OR 1 LITER CARBONATED WATER

1 quart plus 1 cup chilled water, divided

Zest of 1 orange, finely grated

Zest of 1 lemon, finely grated

Zest of 1 lime, finely grated

Pinch ground cinnamon

Pinch ground nutmeg

Pinch ground fennel, or 5–6 whole fennel seeds

¼ teaspoon ground dried ginger

½ cup cherries, stemmed, but not pitted

¼ cup stevia

1 (8" × 16") piece cheesecloth

½ teaspoon vanilla extract

¼ teaspoon almond extract

2 teaspoons brewed strong coffee, chilled

¼ teaspoon citric acid

1. Carbonate 1 quart water with your soda maker, following the manufacturer's directions. Chill on ice or in the refrigerator until cold, about 20 minutes on ice or 1 hour in the fridge.

2. Place remaining water, orange zest, lemon zest, lime zest, cinnamon, nutmeg, fennel, ginger, and cherries into a 1-quart heavy saucepan. Bring to a boil over medium heat. Then simmer, uncovered, for 20 minutes.

3. Remove mixture from heat, stir in stevia, and allow to cool to room temperature, stirring occasionally, about 1 hour. Strain through a wire-mesh sieve, pressing on solids with the back of a wooden spoon to extract as much liquid as possible.

4. If you are happy with how clear the liquid is, skip to the next step. Otherwise, strain a second time: Rinse cheesecloth under cold water. Wring out and fold in half so that you have a square. Line a funnel with cheesecloth. Pour syrup into a storage container through the cheesecloth-lined funnel.

5. Add vanilla extract, almond extract, coffee, and citric acid. Refrigerate mixture until well chilled, about 4 hours.

6. To make cherry cola, place ¼ cup syrup into the bottom of a glass. Add 1 cup chilled carbonated water. Stir gently. Add ice, if desired, and serve.

Tonic Water

The main flavoring in tonic water is quinine, which is derived from the bark of the cinchona tree, native to South America. Luckily, many online retailers sell powdered cinchona bark, enabling you to make delicious tonic water in the comfort of your own kitchen. Don't be surprised if your homemade tonic water is a light tan. The cinchona bark will color the liquid slightly.

MAKES 2 CUPS SYRUP, ENOUGH TO FLAVOR 2 QUARTS OR 2 LITERS CARBONATED WATER

2 quarts plus 2 cups chilled water, divided

1 stalk lemongrass

1 lime

2 cups sugar

¼ cup powdered cinchona bark

2 whole allspice berries

1 (8" × 16") piece cheesecloth

1 teaspoon citric acid

1. Carbonate 2 quarts water with your soda maker, following the manufacturer's directions. Chill on ice or in the refrigerator until cold, about 20 minutes on ice or 1 hour in the fridge.

2. Wash lemongrass stalk. Trim root end off lemongrass and cut lemongrass 4–5" from the bottom, discarding the leafy top. Slice lemongrass in half lengthwise. Remove tough outer layers of lemongrass and discard. Slice soft lemongrass core into ¼" dice. Place into a large saucepot.

3. Using a peeler, remove the zest from the lime, ensuring you remove only the colored part and leave the white behind. Place zest into saucepot with lemongrass.

4. Juice lime into a storage container. Store juice in refrigerator.

5. Add remaining water, sugar, cinchona, and allspice to pot. Bring mixture to a boil and remove from heat. Allow to steep, covered, at room temperature for 30 minutes.

6. Rinse cheesecloth under cold water. Wring out and fold in half so that you have a square. Line a funnel with cheesecloth. Pour syrup into a storage container through the cheesecloth-lined funnel.

7. Stir in citric acid and reserved lime juice. Refrigerate until completely chilled, about 4 hours.

8. To make tonic water, place ¼ cup tonic base into a glass and top with 1 cup carbonated water. Stir gently and serve with ice, if desired.

Sourcing Exotic Ingredients

This Tonic Water recipe calls for cinchona bark. Root Beer lists licorice root as an ingredient. Another soda in this book is based on hibiscus flowers. Where do you find these products? Many natural foods stores have exotic ingredients like these in their spice aisles or in their natural medicine sections. Some spice stores, such as Penzeys in the Midwest, will also carry such ingredients. The national chain Whole Foods Market has some exotic ingredients. It doesn't carry cinchona bark, but will often have licorice root, hibiscus, lavender, and citric acid. If you're having problems finding these ingredients in local stores, try the Internet. Amazon.com carries all of these ingredients and has reviews for each of the products, so you can see what the experiences of other buyers have been. One caveat: When you buy online, you may find that you have to buy in bulk. Not to worry. These ingredients have a long shelf life, typically six months to a year, especially when you store them in airtight containers. Alternately, you can partner with a soda-making friend to split ingredients.

Low-Calorie Tonic Water

Cinchona bark (the main, slightly bitter flavoring in tonic water) and the sweetener stevia grow in the same environment—tropical South America. Here, these two plants come together to create a delicious low-calorie tonic water. Perfect for your next gin and tonic!

**MAKES 2 CUPS SYRUP, ENOUGH TO FLAVOR 2 QUARTS
OR 2 LITERS CARBONATED WATER**

2 quarts plus 2 cups chilled water, divided

1 stalk lemongrass

1 lime

¼ cup powdered cinchona bark

2 whole allspice berries

⅔ cup stevia

1 (8" × 16") piece cheesecloth

1 teaspoon citric acid

1. Carbonate 2 quarts water with your soda maker, following the manufacturer's directions. Chill on ice or in the refrigerator until cold, about 20 minutes on ice or 1 hour in the fridge.

2. Wash lemongrass stalk. Trim root end off lemongrass and cut lemongrass 4–5" from the bottom, discarding the leafy top. Slice lemongrass in half lengthwise. Remove tough outer layers of lemongrass and discard. Slice soft lemongrass core into ¼" dice. Place into a large saucepot.

3. Cut lime in half. Place both halves into saucepot with lemongrass. Add remaining water, cinchona, and allspice. Bring mixture to a boil and remove from heat. Stir in stevia. Allow to steep, covered, at room temperature for 30 minutes. Using tongs, remove lime halves. Squeeze lime juice from each half into the saucepot and discard peels.

4. Rinse cheesecloth under cold water. Wring out and fold in half so that you have a square. Line a funnel with cheesecloth. Pour mixture into a storage container through the cheesecloth-lined funnel.

5. Stir in citric acid. Refrigerate until completely chilled, about 4 hours.

6. To make tonic water, place ¼ cup tonic base into a glass and top with 1 cup carbonated water. Stir gently and serve with ice, if desired.

Lemongrass 101

Lemongrass is a delicious, versatile ingredient that adds distinctive flair to a number of the recipes in this book. It is native to southeast Asia, and is prominently found in Thai and Vietnamese cooking. Luckily, buying lemongrass doesn't require a passport—only a trip to an Asian market or natural foods store. (And in urban areas, it may be in your neighborhood grocery store.) Look for light green stalks that are pliable and free from blemishes. To prepare lemongrass, wash it well and pat it dry. Chop off all but the bottom five inches, discarding the tops. Then peel the rough outer leaves. The inner part contains the most flavor, and is what the recipes in this book call for.

CHAPTER 6

Citrus Sodas

Nothing is more refreshing on a warm day than the combination of citrus and bubbles. With your in-home carbonator, you can enjoy this intoxicating duo at a moment's notice. What's particularly lovely about making citrus soda at home is that you have the opportunity to explore different citrus types, and don't have to rely on the standard lemon-lime or unnaturally bright orange soda you find in stores.

Orange Soda

Store-bought orange soda is a far cry from the fruit itself. Between the intense sweetness and near-neon color, it's hard to know what you're actually drinking! Fortunately, orange soda is one of the easiest soft drinks to make at home. You'll love its muted, natural orange color and restrained sweetness.

**MAKES 1½ CUPS SYRUP, ENOUGH TO FLAVOR 1½ QUARTS
OR 1½ LITERS CARBONATED WATER**

1½ quarts plus ½ cup water, divided
2 oranges (any variety with a thick skin, such as navel, Cara Cara, or blood orange)
½ cup sugar
¼ teaspoon citric acid
Pinch nutmeg

1. Carbonate 1½ quarts water with your soda maker, following the manufacturer's directions. Chill on ice or in the refrigerator until cold, about 20 minutes on ice or 1 hour in the fridge.

2. Using a peeler, remove zest from oranges, ensuring you remove only the colored part and leave the white behind. Place zest into a small saucepot.

3. Juice oranges into a storage container, straining out seeds. Store in refrigerator.

4. Add remaining ½ cup water and sugar to pot. Bring mixture to a boil, reduce heat to simmer, and cook uncovered for 20 minutes.

5. Remove from heat and cool for 20 minutes.

6. Stir in citric acid, nutmeg, and reserved orange juice. Place in a storage container and cool in refrigerator until completely chilled, about 4 hours.

7. To make orange soda, place ¼ cup syrup into the bottom of a glass. Add 1 cup carbonated water and stir gently. Add ice, if desired, and serve.

Low-Calorie Orange Soda

The natural sweetness of orange makes calorie reduction easy in soda recipes. Much of the taste comes from the fruit juice itself, which needs only a hint of sweetener to round out the flavors.

MAKES 1½ CUPS SYRUP, ENOUGH TO FLAVOR 1½ QUARTS OR 1½ LITERS CARBONATED WATER

1½ quarts plus 1 cup water, divided

2 oranges (any variety with a thick skin, such as navel, Cara Cara, or blood orange)

2 tablespoons stevia

¼ teaspoon citric acid

Pinch nutmeg

1. Carbonate 1½ quarts water with your soda maker, following the manufacturer's directions. Chill on ice or in the refrigerator until cold, about 20 minutes on ice or 1 hour in the fridge.

2. Cut oranges in half. Place in a small, heavy saucepan with remaining water and bring to a boil. Reduce heat to simmer, and cook uncovered for 1 hour.

3. Remove from heat. Using tongs, remove orange halves from pot. Squeeze juice from orange halves back into pot and discard peels. Stir in stevia. Cool mixture for 20 minutes.

4. Stir in citric acid and nutmeg. Place in a storage container and cool in refrigerator until completely chilled, about 4 hours.

5. To make orange soda, place ¼ cup syrup into the bottom of a glass. Add 1 cup carbonated water and stir gently. Add ice, if desired, and serve.

Orange Ginger Ale

This citrusy ginger ale relies on fresh juice and fresh ginger, rather than cooked, to create a delicious sparkling drink. If you're in the mood for ginger ale, but don't have the time to take to the stove, consider this fruity alternative.

MAKES 2 CUPS SYRUP, ENOUGH TO FLAVOR ½ QUARTS
OR ½ LITERS CARBONATED WATER

2 cups water, chilled

3 oranges, peeled

1 (1") piece fresh ginger

¼ cup honey

Juice of ½ lemon

1. Carbonate 2 cups water with your soda maker, following the manufacturer's directions. Chill on ice or in the refrigerator until cold, about 20 minutes on ice or 1 hour in the fridge.

2. Process the oranges and the ginger through an electronic juicer according to the manufacturer's directions. Stir in honey and lemon juice. Place in a storage container and cool in refrigerator until completely chilled, about 4 hours.

3. To make soda, place ½ cup syrup into the bottom of a glass. Add ½ cup carbonated water and stir gently. Add ice, if desired, and serve.

Making Juice without a Juicer

This recipe, along with the Kiwi-Apple Soda, call for you to juice fruits and then add them to sparkling water in order to make soda. If you don't have a juicer, you can still make these sodas. Simply wash, seed, peel (if necessary), and cut the fruit. Place the pieces into the bowl of a blender or food processor, add ¼ cup water or fruit juice (for example—orange juice in this recipe, apple juice in the Kiwi-Apple Soda), and puree until there are no more pieces of fruit. This may take a while—3 to 5 minutes—so be patient. Once you have finished puréeing, strain the mixture through a wire-mesh sieve, pressing on solids with the back of a spoon to extract as much liquid as possible. The strained liquid can be used in place of juice that's extracted using a juicer.

Lemon Soda

When you're looking for a break from traditional lemon-lime soda, switch things up and make lemon soda, also known as sparkling lemonade. Carbonated lemonade is also terrific when mixed with other ingredients. For a mocktail, stir in cherry or berry syrup. Or, for a refreshing adult beverage, add your favorite vodka, gin, or rum.

MAKES 1 CUP SYRUP, ENOUGH TO FLAVOR 1 QUART
OR 1 LITER CARBONATED WATER

1 quart plus ½ cup water, divided

3 lemons

½ orange

¾ cup sugar

Pinch salt, preferably a natural salt like kosher or sea salt

1. Carbonate 1 quart water with your soda maker, following the manufacturer's directions. Chill on ice or in the refrigerator until cold, about 20 minutes on ice or 1 hour in the fridge.

2. Using a peeler, remove zest from lemons and orange half, ensuring you remove only the colored part and leave the white behind. Place zest into a small saucepot.

3. Juice lemons into a storage container, straining out seeds. Store in refrigerator. Reserve orange half for another use.

4. Add remaining water, sugar, and salt to pot. Bring mixture to a boil, reduce heat to simmer, and cook uncovered for 20 minutes.

5. Remove from heat and cool for 20 minutes. Strain into storage container.

6. Stir in reserved lemon juice. Cool in refrigerator until completely chilled, about 4 hours.

7. To make lemon soda, place ¼ cup syrup into a glass. Add 1 cup carbonated water. Stir gently. Add ice, if desired, and serve.

Salt Choices

You'll notice that all recipes that call for salt say "preferably a natural salt like kosher or sea salt." But what difference does salt really make? Typically, salt is iodized. This dates back to the nineteenth century, when Americans who lived away from the ocean would get goiters because their diets lacked iodine, an element found in sea salt. Salt manufacturers found that adding iodine to salt that was taken from the earth (rather than from the sea) addressed this nationwide health concern. Now, iodine is regularly added to table salt. The flavor of iodine is somewhat metallic, and can interfere with the flavor of your soda syrups and other foods. For this reason, we recommend that you use kosher salt or sea salt, which lack the added iodine, and therefore also lack the metallic taste.

Low-Calorie Lemon Soda

The method for making reduced-calorie citrus sodas is slightly different than making their sugared cousins. In the sugar version, you make a simple syrup with the zest of the fruit and add in fruit juice. The stevia version calls for simmering halved fruits for an hour, which enables you to pull flavor from the zest and the juice at the same time, without the use of sugar.

MAKES 1 CUP SYRUP, ENOUGH TO FLAVOR 1 QUART OR 1 LITER CARBONATED WATER

1 quart plus ½ cup water, divided

3 lemons

½ orange

Pinch salt, preferably a natural salt like kosher or sea salt

2 tablespoons stevia

1. Carbonate 1 quart water with your soda maker, following the manufacturer's directions. Chill on ice or in the refrigerator until cold, about 20 minutes on ice or 1 hour in the fridge.

2. Cut lemons in half. Place into a heavy saucepot with remaining water, orange half, and salt. Bring mixture to a boil, reduce heat to simmer, and cook uncovered for 1 hour.

3. Remove from heat. Using tongs, remove lemon and orange halves from pot. Squeeze juice from both citrus fruits back into pot, straining out seeds. Discard peels. Stir in stevia. Cool mixture for 20 minutes. Place in a storage container and cool in refrigerator until completely chilled, about 4 hours.

4. To make lemon soda, place ¼ cup syrup into a glass. Add 1 cup carbonated water. Stir gently. Add ice, if desired, and serve.

Lime Soda

Whether you use large Persian limes (the limes commonly sold in grocery stores) or tiny Key limes, you'll love the crispness of your own carbonated limeade. The addition of small quantities of bay leaf, thyme, and lemon juice round out the flavors of the lime.

**MAKES 1 CUP SYRUP, ENOUGH TO FLAVOR 1 QUART
OR 1 LITER CARBONATED WATER**

1 quart plus ½ cup water, divided

6 large limes, or 20 Key limes

1 cup sugar

1 dried bay leaf

Pinch dried thyme

2 tablespoons lemon juice

1. Carbonate 1 quart water with your soda maker, following the manufacturer's directions. Chill on ice or in the refrigerator until cold, about 20 minutes on ice or 1 hour in the fridge.

2. Using a peeler, remove zest from limes, ensuring you remove only the green part and leave the white behind. Place zest into a small saucepot.

3. Juice limes into a storage container, straining out seeds. Store in refrigerator.

4. Add remaining water, sugar, bay leaf, and thyme to pot. Bring mixture to a boil, reduce heat to simmer, and cook uncovered for 20 minutes.

5. Remove from heat and cool for 20 minutes. Strain into storage container.

6. Stir in reserved lime juice and lemon juice. Cool in refrigerator until completely chilled, about 4 hours.

7. To make lime soda, place ¼ cup syrup into a glass. Add 1 cup chilled carbonated water. Stir gently. Add ice, if desired, and serve.

Persian Limes vs. Key Limes

Typical large grocery-store limes are called "Persian limes." They are large, dark green, and decidedly tart. Key limes, on the other hand, are about the diameter of a quarter, with yellowish-green skin. Persian limes have a hint of pine or rosemary on the palate, whereas Key limes are a bit sweeter. Usually, Persian limes are easier to find and much cheaper. However, if you live in a tropical climate, the opposite is likely to be true. In places like the Caribbean and Florida (as well as throughout Asia and the Middle East), Key limes are more common.

Low-Calorie Lime Soda

Although you can make this drink with whatever limes you have on hand, Key limes are especially nice in the low-calorie version. Because they are slightly sweeter, they blend well with the taste of the stevia. The only downside is that you will have more lime pieces to squeeze.

MAKES 1 CUP SYRUP, ENOUGH TO FLAVOR 1 QUART OR 1 LITER CARBONATED WATER

1 quart plus ½ cup water, divided

6 large limes, or 20 Key limes

1 dried bay leaf

Pinch dried thyme

¼ cup stevia

2 tablespoons lemon juice

1. Carbonate 1 quart water with your soda maker, following the manufacturer's directions. Chill on ice or in the refrigerator until cold, about 20 minutes on ice or 1 hour in the fridge.

2. Cut limes in half. Place into a small saucepot. Add remaining water, bay leaf, and thyme to pot. Bring mixture to a boil, reduce heat to simmer, and cook uncovered for 1 hour.

3. Remove from heat. Using tongs, remove lime halves from pot. Squeeze juice from limes back into pot, straining out seeds. Discard peels. Stir in stevia. Cool mixture for 20 minutes. Stir in lemon juice. Place in a storage container and cool in refrigerator until completely chilled, about 4 hours.

4. To make lime soda, place ¼ cup syrup into a glass. Add 1 cup chilled carbonated water. Stir gently. Add ice, if desired, and serve.

Grapefruit Soda

The slight bitterness of grapefruit rind, combined with tart grapefruit juice and just a hint of carbonation, makes for a mouthwatering combination. Although this is delicious with any grapefruit variety, it looks prettiest when made with pink or ruby red grapefruits.

MAKES 2 CUPS SYRUP, ENOUGH TO FLAVOR 2 QUARTS OR 2 LITERS CARBONATED WATER

2 quarts plus 1 cup water, divided

2 whole grapefruits (any variety you like—pink, white, yellow, or ruby red)

1 cup sugar

⅛ teaspoon salt, preferably a natural salt like kosher or sea salt

Pinch dried rosemary

Juice of ½ lemon

1. Carbonate 2 quarts water with your soda maker, following the manufacturer's directions. Chill on ice or in the refrigerator until cold, about 20 minutes on ice or 1 hour in the fridge.

2. Using a peeler, remove zest from grapefruit, ensuring you remove only the colored part and leave the white behind. Place zest into a small saucepot.

3. Juice grapefruit into a storage container, straining out seeds. Store in refrigerator.

4. Add remaining water, sugar, salt, and rosemary to pot. Bring mixture to a boil, reduce heat to simmer, and cook uncovered for 20 minutes.

5. Remove from heat and cool for 20 minutes. Strain into storage container.

6. Stir in reserved grapefruit juice and lemon juice. Cool in refrigerator until completely chilled, about 4 hours.

7. To make grapefruit soda, place ¼ cup syrup into a glass. Add 1 cup chilled carbonated water. Stir gently. Add ice, if desired, and serve.

Low-Calorie Grapefruit Soda

The low-calorie version of this beverage is as delicious as the sugared version, which is probably why low-calorie grapefruit soda (sometimes known as Fresca) is so easy to find in stores. With this recipe, you can change the look and taste of the soda simply by using different varieties of grapefruits.

MAKES 2 CUPS SYRUP, ENOUGH TO FLAVOR 2 QUARTS OR 2 LITERS CARBONATED WATER

2 quarts plus 1 cup water, divided

2 whole grapefruits (any variety you like—pink, white, yellow, or ruby red)

⅛ teaspoon salt, preferably a natural salt like kosher or sea salt

Pinch dried rosemary

⅓ cup stevia

Juice of ½ lemon

1. Carbonate 2 quarts water with your soda maker, following the manufacturer's directions. Chill on ice or in the refrigerator until cold, about 20 minutes on ice or 1 hour in the fridge.

2. Using a peeler, remove zest from grapefruit, ensuring you remove only the colored part and leave the white behind. Place zest into a small saucepot.

3. Juice grapefruit into a storage container, straining out seeds. Store in refrigerator.

4. Add remaining water, salt, and rosemary to pot. Bring mixture to a boil, reduce heat to simmer, and cook uncovered for 20 minutes.

5. Remove from heat, stir in stevia, and cool for 20 minutes. Strain into storage container.

6. Stir in reserved grapefruit juice and lemon juice. Cool in refrigerator until completely chilled, about 4 hours.

7. To make grapefruit soda, place ¼ cup syrup into a glass. Add 1 cup chilled carbonated water. Stir gently. Add ice, if desired, and serve.

Tangerine Soda

Think tangerines are simply overly sweet oranges? Think again. This citrusy gem, while definitely sweeter than an orange, has a spicy appeal all its own. One of the best ways to enjoy the subtleties of tangerines is by making them into soda. Gentle carbonation will clean your palate, letting you taste all the intricacies this fruit contains.

MAKES 1 CUP SYRUP, ENOUGH TO FLAVOR 1 QUART OR 1 LITER CARBONATED WATER

1 quart plus ½ cup water, divided

2 tangerines

¼ cup sugar

¼ cup honey

Pinch nutmeg

Pinch cinnamon

1. Carbonate 1 quart water with your soda maker, following the manufacturer's directions. Chill on ice or in the refrigerator until cold, about 20 minutes on ice or 1 hour in the fridge.

2. Using a microplane or the small holes on a box grater, remove zest from tangerines, ensuring you remove only the colored part and leave the white behind. Place zest into a small saucepot.

3. Juice tangerines into a storage container, straining out seeds. Store in refrigerator.

4. Add remaining water, sugar, honey, nutmeg, and cinnamon to pot. Bring mixture to a boil, reduce heat to simmer, and cook uncovered for 20 minutes.

5. Remove from heat and cool for 20 minutes. Stir in reserved tangerine juice. Strain into a storage container and cool in refrigerator until completely chilled, about 4 hours.

6. To make tangerine soda, place ¼ cup syrup into a glass. Add 1 cup carbonated water and stir gently. Add ice, if desired, and serve.

Low-Calorie Tangerine Soda

Unlike other low-calorie versions of sodas in this cookbook, this tangerine soda simply eliminates all of the sugar and doesn't replace any with stevia. Instead, a small amount of honey brings out the flavor of the fruit, and sweetens it all at once.

MAKES 1 CUP SYRUP, ENOUGH TO FLAVOR 1 QUART OR 1 LITER CARBONATED WATER

1 quart plus ½ cup water, divided

2 tangerines

2 tablespoons honey

Pinch nutmeg

Pinch cinnamon

1. Carbonate 1 quart water with your soda maker, following the manufacturer's directions. Chill on ice or in the refrigerator until cold, about 20 minutes on ice or 1 hour in the fridge.

2. Cut tangerines in half and place in a heavy saucepot. Add remaining water, honey, nutmeg, and cinnamon to pot. Bring mixture to a boil, reduce heat to simmer, and cook uncovered for 1 hour.

3. Remove from heat. Using tongs, remove tangerine halves from pot. Squeeze juice from tangerines back into pot, straining out seeds. Discard peels. Cool mixture for 20 minutes. Place in a storage container and cool in refrigerator until completely chilled, about 4 hours.

4. To make tangerine soda, place ¼ cup syrup into a glass. Add 1 cup carbonated water and stir gently. Add ice, if desired, and serve.

CHAPTER 7

Cherry, Grape, and Berry Sodas

By making soda in your kitchen with sweet berries, cherries, and grapes, you'll infuse nature's sweetest treasures with a hint of sparkle. Kids tend to love these flavors, so you might find yourself with a kitchen full of taste-testers!

Cherry Soda

It's easy to fall in love with cherry soda. The rich color and heady sweetness are offset by a cascade of bubbles, making for a very celebratory quaff. In this recipe, you'll add clove and almond extract, which really bring out the spicier notes in cherries. Leaving the pits in while cooking the cherry syrup also enhances the cherry flavor. Although this recipe calls for sour cherries, you can substitute sweet cherries. Simply reduce the amount of sugar to ¼ cup.

**MAKES 3 CUPS SYRUP, ENOUGH TO FLAVOR 3 LITERS
OR 3 QUARTS CARBONATED WATER**

3 quarts plus 2 cups water, divided
2 pounds sour cherries, washed and stemmed, pits left in
1 cup white sugar
2–3 whole cloves
½ teaspoon almond extract

1. Carbonate 3 quarts water with your soda maker, following the manufacturer's directions. Chill on ice or in the refrigerator until cold, about 20 minutes on ice or 1 hour in the fridge.

2. Place cherries, remaining water, sugar, and cloves in a medium saucepan. Bring to a boil over medium heat. Reduce heat and simmer, uncovered, until cherries burst, about 30 minutes.

3. Remove from heat and strain mixture through a wire-mesh sieve, pressing on solids with the back of a wooden spoon to extract as much liquid as possible. Allow to cool to room temperature, about 1 hour.

4. Stir in almond extract. Pour syrup into a storage container and chill until completely cold, about 4 hours.

5. To make cherry soda, place ¼ cup syrup into the bottom of a glass. Add 1 cup chilled carbonated water. Stir gently. Add ice, if desired, and serve.

Add Cherry Syrup to Other Drinks

Cherry syrup is incredibly versatile and can add a different flavor dimension to other soft drinks. Try a few teaspoons in Cola, Lemon-Lime Soda, or Ginger Ale to replicate the cherry-kissed flavors you find in stores. Or, add cherry syrup to citrus sodas, such as lemon, grapefruit, lime, or orange. For an especially attractive presentation, place a few teaspoons of cherry syrup at the bottom of a glass and fill with a light-colored soda, but don't stir. The bottom of your drink will be deep red, and the drink will diffuse to light pink at the top.

Low-Calorie Cherry Soda

Like the regular Cherry Soda recipe, this low-calorie version calls for sour cherries. And like the regular recipe, this version readily adapts to sweet cherries. If you use sweet cherries, eliminate the stevia altogether.

**MAKES 3 CUPS SYRUP, ENOUGH TO FLAVOR 3 LITERS
OR 3 QUARTS CARBONATED WATER**

3 quarts plus 2 cups water, divided
2 pounds sour cherries, washed and stemmed, pits left in
2–3 whole cloves
¼ cup stevia
½ teaspoon almond extract

1. Carbonate 3 quarts water with your soda maker, following the manufacturer's directions. Chill on ice or in the refrigerator until cold, about 20 minutes on ice or 1 hour in the fridge.

2. Place cherries, remaining water, and cloves in a medium saucepan. Bring to a boil over medium heat. Reduce heat and simmer, uncovered, until cherries burst, about 30 minutes.

3. Remove from heat and strain mixture through a wire-mesh sieve, pressing on solids with the back of a wooden spoon to extract as much liquid as possible. Stir in stevia. Allow to cool to room temperature, about 1 hour.

4. Stir in almond extract. Pour syrup into a storage container and chill until completely cold, about 4 hours.

5. To make cherry soda, place ¼ cup syrup into the bottom of a glass. Add 1 cup chilled carbonated water. Stir gently. Add ice, if desired, and serve.

Grape Soda

Whereas grapes are the perfect mix of sweet and tangy, most grape soda has the shocking flavor of cough syrup. Ditch the chemical flavors and make your own. Start with unsweetened grape juice and end with a smile.

MAKES 1 CUP SYRUP, ENOUGH TO FLAVOR 1 QUART OR 1 LITER CARBONATED WATER

1 quart water

3 cups bottled unsweetened grape juice

¼ cup fresh or frozen blueberries

2 tablespoons sugar

Pinch salt, preferably a natural salt like kosher or sea salt

1 tablespoon fresh lemon juice

Pinch ground cinnamon

1. Carbonate 1 quart water with your soda maker, following the manufacturer's directions. Chill on ice or in the refrigerator until cold, about 20 minutes on ice or 1 hour in the fridge.

2. Place grape juice, blueberries, sugar, and salt into a large, heavy saucepot. Bring to a boil over high heat.

3. Reduce heat to medium and simmer uncovered until mixture is reduced by ¾, about 45 minutes to 1 hour.

4. Remove from heat and strain mixture through a wire-mesh sieve, pressing on solids with the back of a wooden spoon to extract as much liquid as possible. Stir in lemon juice and cinnamon. Allow to cool to room temperature, about 1 hour.

5. Pour syrup into a storage container and chill until completely cold, about 4 hours.

6. To make grape soda, place ¼ cup syrup into the bottom of a glass. Add 1 cup chilled carbonated water. Stir gently. Add ice, if desired, and serve.

A Touch of the Blues

This recipe calls for blueberries to be added. The reason is two-fold. First, blueberries round out the color of grape juice, adding an appealing deep blue color, which will either tint white grape juice or round out the color of red grape juice, making it more purple. Also, blueberries balance the sweetness in grapes. No blueberries on hand? No problem! This recipe is just fine without them.

Jam on It

Looking for a way to make a no-added-sugar grape jam? Use this recipe for grape soda, but increase the quantity of blueberries from ¼ cup to 1 cup. You'll find that the grape mixture is the consistency of jelly after the adjusted recipe chills. This is thanks to the natural pectin found in blueberries.

Strawberry Soda

This is a great way to use strawberries when early summer brings a large harvest of strawberries. A delicate and blushing soda, strawberry soda is the perfect guest at any party and complements the flavor of summery foods, such as barbecued chicken and grilled vegetables. If you like a more exotic drink, add a few drops of rose water to the soda as you serve it.

MAKES ROUGHLY 2 CUPS SYRUP, ENOUGH TO FLAVOR 1 QUART OR 1 LITER CARBONATED WATER

1 quart plus ½ cup water, divided

2 pounds fresh or frozen strawberries

1 cup sugar

Zest of 1 lemon, removed in large pieces with a vegetable peeler

Pinch dried mint

2–3 whole allspice berries

Apple Cider
Smash

Chapter 11

Cherry
Soda

Chapter 7

In
the Pink
Sparkling
Lemonade
Chapter 10

Classic
Root Beer
Float
Chapter 10

Strawberry
Soda
Chapter 7

Orange
Soda
Chapter 6

Cranberry
Soda

Chapter 7

Lime-
Grapefruit
Chiller with
Mint
Chapter 10

15 Col

Lime Soda
Chapter 6

(left to right:)

Pineapple Cilantro Soda
Chapter 9

Orange Ginger Ale *Chapter 6*

Mixed-Berry Soda *Chapter 7*

Strawberry Soda *Chapter 7*

Lemongrass Soda
Chapter 9

Watermelon
Soda

Chapter 8

Peach Soda

Chapter 8

Tangerine Soda

Chapter 6

Sangria

Chapter 11

Lavender
Soda

Chapter 9

Sparkling
Pomegranate

Chapter 7

Hibiscus
Soda

Chapter 9

1. Carbonate 1 quart water with your soda maker, following the manufacturer's directions. Chill on ice or in the refrigerator until cold, about 20 minutes on ice or 1 hour in the fridge.

2. Wash berries and remove stems and leaves. Place berries into the bowl of a blender or food processor and blend until smooth, about 3 minutes.

3. Place a wire-mesh sieve over a medium saucepan. Strain berry mixture through sieve, pressing on the mixture with the back of a wooden spoon to extract as much liquid as possible.

4. Add remaining water, sugar, lemon zest, mint, and allspice to saucepan. Bring to a boil over medium heat. Then simmer, uncovered, until reduced by half, about 15 minutes.

5. Remove syrup from heat. Remove lemon zest and allspice berries. Allow to cool to room temperature, stirring occasionally, about 1 hour. Pour syrup into a storage container and chill until completely cold, about 4 hours.

6. To make strawberry soda, place ½ cup syrup into the bottom of a glass. Add 1 cup chilled carbonated water. Stir gently. Add ice, if desired, and serve.

Low-Calorie Strawberry Soda

Roasting berries? Yes! This reduced-calorie soda (as well as Low-Calorie Mixed-Berry Soda) uses oven roasting as a technique for coaxing out the natural sweetness of strawberries. By baking in a hot oven, the strawberries release water, thereby concentrating their flavor. The dry heat also caramelizes the natural fruit sugars, making them taste sweeter. Plus, roasting helps the zest and allspice release essential oils, which is where the flavor is concentrated. Once you make this base, you may find that you prefer it to be sweeter. If that's the case, add stevia 1 teaspoon at a time to the base, making glasses of soda with the stevia-sweetened base to test whether the sweetness level is to your liking.

**MAKES ROUGHLY 2 CUPS SYRUP, ENOUGH TO FLAVOR 1 QUART
OR 1 LITER CARBONATED WATER**

1 quart water

2 pounds fresh or frozen strawberries

Zest of 1 lemon, removed in large pieces with a vegetable peeler

Pinch dried mint

2–3 whole allspice berries

1. Preheat oven to 425°F.

2. Carbonate 1 quart water with your soda maker, following the manufacturer's directions. Chill on ice or in the refrigerator until cold, about 20 minutes on ice or 1 hour in the fridge.

3. Wash berries and remove stems and leaves. Chop into quarters. Place berries onto a rimmed baking sheet, along with the lemon zest, mint, and allspice. Roast until strawberries release their juice, about 10–15 minutes. (This may take up to 20 minutes if you start with frozen berries.)

4. Remove from oven and cool until the berries are a temperature you're comfortable handling.

5. Place a wire-mesh sieve over the bowl of a blender or food processor. Strain berry mixture and any pan juices through sieve, pressing on the mixture with the back of a wooden spoon to extract as much liquid as possible.

6. Pulse 3–4 times to release steam. Then purée on high until smooth, about 1 minute.

7. Transfer to a storage container and chill until completely cold, about 4 hours.

8. To make strawberry soda, place ½ cup syrup into the bottom of a glass. Add 1 cup chilled carbonated water. Stir gently. Add ice, if desired, and serve.

Do I Need to Defrost Frozen Fruit?

Using frozen fruit is a great way to create fruity soda bases. Frozen fruit is often sweeter and more flavorful than fresh fruit, because it's picked in season, and flash frozen. When making soda base recipes, you do not need to thaw fruits before cooking. Cooking will defrost the fruit naturally. In recipes where you simmer fruit, it will simply take a little longer for the fruit to come to a boil. For recipes where you roast fruit, you will add a few minutes at the end of the roasting time to achieve desired results. For cocktails and nonalcoholic drinks, you *will* have to defrost the fruit. To do so, pour the recipe amount into a bowl and leave on your kitchen counter for a half hour. Be sure to keep the liquid that surrounds the fruit and add it to your recipe. You don't want to lose a drop of flavor!

Mixed-Berry Soda

Capture the sunny essence of a summer day by making mixed-berry soda. Choose the proportions of berries based on your tastes, and what looks best in the marketplace. If you can't find delicious-looking fresh berries, feel free to substitute frozen berries. These are often picked and frozen in the height of summer, making them the perfect candidates to go into a flavorful soda.

MAKES 3 CUPS SYRUP, ENOUGH TO FLAVOR 3 QUARTS
OR 3 LITERS CARBONATED WATER

3 quarts plus 1 cup chilled water, divided

2 pounds mixed fresh or frozen berries (may include strawberries, blueberries, raspberries, blackberries, currants, and/or cranberries)

1 cup sugar, divided

½ lemon

Pinch ground cinnamon

Pinch dried basil

1. Carbonate 3 quarts water with your soda maker, following the manufacturer's directions. Chill on ice or in the refrigerator until cold, about 20 minutes on ice or 1 hour in the fridge.

2. Wash berries and remove stems and leaves. Place berries into the bowl of a blender or food processor and sprinkle with 1 tablespoon sugar. Let berries sit 3–5 minutes to release their juices. Blend until smooth, about 3 minutes.

3. Place a wire-mesh sieve over a medium saucepan. Strain berry mixture through sieve, pressing on the mixture with the back of a wooden spoon to extract as much liquid as possible.

4. Using a vegetable peeler, remove zest from lemon half in long strips, taking care to remove only yellow part. Juice lemon half and strain into a container. Place in refrigerator.

5. Add remaining sugar, zest, and 1 cup water to saucepan. Bring to a boil over medium heat. Then simmer, uncovered, until reduced by half, about 15 minutes.

6. Remove syrup from heat and stir in cinnamon and basil. Allow to cool to room temperature, stirring occasionally, about 1 hour. Add reserved lemon juice and pour syrup into a storage container. Chill until completely cold, about 4 hours.

7. To make berry soda, place ¼ cup syrup into a glass. Top with 1 cup chilled carbonated water. Stir gently. Add ice, if desired, and serve.

Low-Calorie Mixed-Berry Soda

One of the joys of making a mixed-fruit soda is that it will be different every time, depending on what you have on hand, or what you find for the least amount of money at the market. With this low-calorie version, be sure to take good notes—some combinations of berries may require more sweetener than others. Always start with the smallest amount of sweetener, then increase to taste when you mix the syrup with carbonated water.

MAKES 2 CUPS SYRUP, ENOUGH TO FLAVOR 1½ QUARTS
OR 1½ LITERS CARBONATED WATER

2 quarts chilled water

2 pounds mixed fresh or frozen berries (may include strawberries, blueberries, raspberries, blackberries, currants, and/or cranberries)

½ lemon

Pinch ground cinnamon

Pinch dried basil

1–2 tablespoons stevia, or to taste

1. Preheat oven to 425°F.

2. Carbonate 2 quarts water with your soda maker, following the manufacturer's directions. Chill on ice or in the refrigerator until cold, about 20 minutes on ice or 1 hour in the fridge.

3. Wash berries and remove stems and leaves. Spread berries in an even layer on a rimmed baking sheet.

4. Using a vegetable peeler, remove zest from lemon half in long strips, taking care to remove only yellow part. Add zest to berry mixture and sprinkle with cinnamon and basil.

5. Juice lemon half and strain into a container. Place in refrigerator.

6. Roast berries until their juices run out, about 10–15 minutes. (This may take up to 20 minutes if you start with frozen berries.)

7. Place a wire-mesh sieve over the bowl of a blender or food processor. Strain berry mixture and any pan juices through sieve, pressing on the mixture with the back of a wooden spoon to extract as much liquid as possible.

8. Add 1 tablespoon stevia, and pulse 3–4 times to release steam. Then purée on high until smooth, about 1 minute.

9. Transfer to a storage container and chill until completely cold, about 4 hours.

10. To make berry soda, place ¼ cup syrup into the bottom of a glass. Add 1 cup chilled carbonated water. Stir gently. Add ice, if desired, and serve.

Sparkling Pomegranate Soda

Making sparkling pomegranate soda from scratch is quite a job—the work of juicing a pomegranate is a tedious mess. Now, thankfully, several juice processors sell pomegranate juice in the produce section of your local grocer. That means that this sparkling beverage is quick and easy to make. If you want to add the feel of a whole fresh pomegranate to this drink, just sprinkle a few seeds over the finished product as a garnish.

MAKES 1 CUP SYRUP, ENOUGH TO FLAVOR 1 LITER OR 1 QUART CARBONATED WATER

1 quart chilled water
4 cups pomegranate juice
2–3 whole black peppercorns
Juice of 1 lime

1. Carbonate 1 quart water with your soda maker, following the manufacturer's directions. Chill on ice or in the refrigerator until cold, about 20 minutes on ice or 1 hour in the fridge.

2. Place pomegranate juice and peppercorns into a large, heavy saucepot. Bring to a boil over high heat.

3. Reduce heat to medium and simmer uncovered until mixture is reduced by ¾, about 30–35 minutes.

4. Remove from heat and strain mixture through a wire-mesh sieve. Allow to cool to room temperature, about 1 hour. Stir in lime juice. Transfer to a storage container and chill until completely cold, about 4 hours.

5. To make pomegranate soda, place ¼ cup syrup into the bottom of a glass. Add 1 cup chilled carbonated water. Stir gently. Add ice, if desired, and serve.

Cranberry Soda

Ah, the humble cranberry. It's often relegated to a Thanksgiving side dish or the best friend of vodka in a Cosmopolitan, yet it has so much more to offer! The best cranberries have a bright sourness, with a hint of pine and citrus. With the judicious addition of sugar and carbonation, you can uncover the hidden flavors of cranberry that reveal themselves in a refreshing soda.

MAKES 1 CUP SYRUP, ENOUGH TO FLAVOR 1 QUART OR 1 LITER CARBONATED WATER

1 quart water

6 cups bottled cranberry juice, preferably sweetened with juice

½ orange, cut into pieces

Pinch Kosher salt

Juice of ½ lemon

1. Carbonate 1 quart water with your soda maker, following the manufacturer's directions. Chill on ice or in the refrigerator until cold, about 20 minutes on ice or 1 hour in the fridge.

2. Place cranberry juice, orange pieces, and salt into a medium saucepan. Bring to a boil over medium heat. Reduce heat and simmer, uncovered, until mixture reduces by ⅔ (you should have 2 cups), about 35–40 minutes.

3. Remove from heat and strain mixture through a wire-mesh sieve, pressing on solids with the back of a wooden spoon to extract as much liquid as possible. Stir in lemon juice. Allow to cool to room temperature, stirring often, about 1 hour.

4. Pour syrup into a storage container and chill until completely cold, about 4 hours.

5. To make cranberry soda, place ½ cup syrup into the bottom of a glass. Add 1 cup chilled carbonated water. Stir gently. Add ice, if desired, and serve.

Low-Calorie Cranberry Soda

The natural tartness of cranberries makes it necessary to sweeten them. In this recipe, orange mellows the tart flavor, and a little stevia sweetens the drink so it's deliciously refreshing.

MAKES 2 CUPS SYRUP, ENOUGH TO FLAVOR 1 QUART OR 1 LITER CARBONATED WATER

1 quart plus 2 cups water, divided
12 ounces fresh or frozen cranberries
1 orange, cut in half
⅓ cup stevia
Juice of ½ lemon

1. Carbonate 1 quart water with your soda maker, following the manufacturer's directions. Chill on ice or in the refrigerator until cold, about 20 minutes on ice or 1 hour in the fridge.

2. Wash cranberries and place them, along with remaining water and orange halves, into a medium saucepan. Bring to a boil over medium heat. Reduce heat and simmer, uncovered, until cranberries "pop" and burst open, about 30 minutes.

3. Remove from heat and strain mixture through a wire-mesh sieve, pressing on solids with the back of a wooden spoon to extract as much liquid as possible. Stir in stevia and lemon juice, and allow to cool to room temperature, stirring often, about 1 hour.

4. Pour syrup into a storage container and chill until completely cold, about 4 hours.

5. To make cranberry soda, place ½ cup syrup into the bottom of a glass. Add 1 cup chilled carbonated water. Stir gently. Add ice, if desired, and serve.

CHAPTER 8

Other Fruit Sodas

While the grocery store carries standard sodas—cola, lemon-lime, grape, and orange—it's a challenge to find other options, like pineapple, mango, or pear. Enter home soda-making! With nature's ripest produce, a little time, and a handful of other ingredients, you can enjoy your favorite fruit as a carbonated beverage.

Sour Apple Soda

Store-bought varieties of sour apple soda are an unnatural green, making you wonder how the bottler makes the color. You can rest assured when you make sour apple soda at home. You get all the flavor you love with none of the additives that make it a shocking green.

MAKES 2 CUPS SYRUP, ENOUGH TO FLAVOR 1 QUART OR 1 LITER CARBONATED WATER

1 quart plus ½ cup chilled water, divided

⅔ cup sugar

1 long, wide strip lemon zest, yellow part only

4 medium tart apples, such as Granny Smith or McIntosh

½ teaspoon citric acid

1. Carbonate 1 quart water with your soda maker, following the manufacturer's directions. Chill on ice or in the refrigerator until cold, about 20 minutes on ice or 1 hour in the fridge.

2. Place remaining water, sugar, and zest into a saucepot. Bring to a boil and cook until sugar has dissolved, about 3 minutes.

3. Wash apples, remove stems, and cut in half. Using a melon baller, remove seed packs from apples, discarding seeds. Roughly chop apples and place in a bowl. Pour hot sugar solution over apples, cover bowl tightly, and place in refrigerator. Chill for at least 4 hours.

4. Puree mixture in a blender or food processor. Strain mixture through a wire-mesh strainer, pressing on solids with the back of a spoon to extract as much of the liquid as possible. Stir in citric acid. Transfer syrup to a storage container and chill until completely cold, about 4 hours.

5. To make soda, place ½ cup syrup into a glass. Top with 1 cup sparkling water and stir gently. Add ice, if desired, and serve.

Low-Calorie Sour Apple Soda

This is one of the few "fresh" soda recipes in this book, meaning you don't cook the ingredients before turning them into a base. For this reason, make sure you keep this base well chilled, and adhere to its freshness date strictly. The added lemon juice and citric acid work as natural preservatives, so this base will still last for two weeks in your refrigerator. If the soda is not sweet enough for you, add up to 1 additional tablespoon of stevia to the base.

**MAKES 2 CUPS SYRUP, ENOUGH TO FLAVOR 1 QUART
OR 1 LITER CARBONATED WATER**

1 quart plus ½ cup chilled water, divided

4 medium tart apples, such as Granny Smith or McIntosh

2 tablespoons lemon juice

1–2 tablespoons stevia

½ teaspoon citric acid

1. Carbonate 1 quart water with your soda maker, following the manufacturer's directions. Chill on ice or in the refrigerator until cold, about 20 minutes on ice or 1 hour in the fridge.

2. Wash apples, remove stems, and cut in half. Using a melon baller, remove seed packs from apples, discarding seeds. Roughly chop apples and place into the bowl of a blender or food processor. Add remaining water and lemon juice, and purée on high until completely smooth, about 3 minutes.

3. Strain mixture through a wire-mesh strainer, pressing on solids with the back of a spoon to extract as much of the liquid as possible. Stir in 1 tablespoon stevia and citric acid. Transfer syrup to a storage container and chill until completely cold, about 4 hours.

4. To make soda, place ½ cup syrup into a glass. Top with 1 cup sparkling water and stir gently. Add ice, if desired, and serve.

Pear Soda

When ripe pears are in season, you really have to capitalize on them—unlike apples, pears don't keep well after picking. The next time you find yourself with an abundance of pears, whip up some pear syrup. Not only is it a delicious base for soda; it's also a great substitute for apple butter.

MAKES 2⅔ CUPS SYRUP, ENOUGH TO FLAVOR 2 QUARTS OR 2 LITERS CARBONATED WATER

2 quarts plus 1 cup water, divided

Zest from ½ lemon, removed in large strips

½ cup sugar

6 fresh pears, stemmed, seeded, and coarsely chopped

1 teaspoon whole black peppercorns

Pinch nutmeg

Pinch ground allspice

1. Carbonate 2 quarts water with your soda maker, following the manufacturer's directions. Chill on ice or in the refrigerator until cold, about 20 minutes on ice or 1 hour in the fridge.

2. Add remaining water, zest, sugar, pears, peppercorns, nutmeg, and allspice to saucepot. Bring to a boil over medium heat. Reduce heat and simmer covered for 45–50 minutes.

3. Strain mixture through a wire-mesh sieve, pressing on solids with the back of a wooden spoon to remove as much liquid as possible.

4. Transfer syrup to a storage container and chill until completely cold, about 4 hours.

5. To make soda, place ⅓ cup syrup into a glass. Top with 1 cup sparkling water and stir gently. Add ice, if desired, and serve.

Pear Types for Delicious Sodas

With the variety of pears on the market—from Bosc to Comice to Anjou—you may wonder which pear is best for soda. The answer to that depends on your tastes. Firmer pear varieties, such as Bosc, are generally tarter in flavor and will yield a drier soda. Juicier pears, like Anjou, tend to have flavors of baking spices, like cinnamon and nutmeg. These flavors add a subtle depth to homemade soda. Either type of pear is suitable as a soda base. Because this recipe calls for cooking the pears in order to turn them into syrup, either firm or juicy pears turn into a silky syrup.

Low-Calorie Pear Soda

Roasting the pear adds a caramel flavor, which makes the soda taste more complex. You might even want to try roasting the pear when making the sugar version of this recipe! If you make this recipe with sugar, instead of stevia, use ½ cup of sugar and sprinkle it on the pears before you roast them.

**MAKES 2 CUPS SYRUP, ENOUGH TO FLAVOR 1 QUART
OR 1 LITER CARBONATED WATER**

2 quarts plus 1 cup water, divided

6 fresh pears, stemmed, seeded, and coarsely chopped

Zest from ½ lemon, removed in large strips

¼ teaspoon ground black pepper

Pinch nutmeg

Pinch ground allspice

1–4 tablespoons stevia, optional

1. Preheat oven to 425°F.

2. Carbonate 1 quart water with your soda maker, following the manufacturer's directions. Chill on ice or in the refrigerator until cold, about 20 minutes on ice or 1 hour in the fridge.

3. Place pears and lemon zest onto a rimmed baking sheet. Sprinkle with pepper, nutmeg, and allspice. Roast until pears soften, releasing their juices, and the juices are bubbling, about 35–40 minutes.

4. Remove from oven and cool until comfortable enough to handle. Remove lemon zest and discard.

5. Strain pears, along with pan juices, into the bowl of a food processor or blender. Add remaining water and optional stevia, and pulse 3–4 times to let off steam. Then purée on high until smooth, about 2–3 minutes. Strain through a wire-mesh sieve, pressing on solids with the back of a wooden spoon to remove as much liquid as possible.

6. Transfer syrup to a storage container and chill until completely cold, about 4 hours.

7. To make soda, place ½ cup syrup into a glass. Top with 1 cup sparkling water and stir gently. Add ice, if desired, and serve.

Peach Soda

This peach soda is like drinking the ripest, juiciest peach that's fizzing with flavor. The honey and lemon in this recipe round out the peachy flavor. Perfect for drinking with Cola-Brined Fried Chicken (see Chapter 12) or any of your favorite Southern recipes.

**MAKES 2 CUPS SYRUP, ENOUGH TO FLAVOR 1 QUART
OR 1 LITER CARBONATED WATER**

2 quarts plus 1 cup water, divided

½ lemon

½ cup sugar

½ cup honey

4 fresh peaches, peeled, pitted, and coarsely chopped, or 2 cups unsweetened frozen peaches

Pinch nutmeg

1. Carbonate 1 quart water with your soda maker, following the manufacturer's directions. Chill on ice or in the refrigerator until cold, about 20 minutes on ice or 1 hour in the fridge.

2. Using a microplane or the smallest holes on a box grater, grate zest from lemon half into a small saucepot, taking care to remove only the yellow part.

3. Squeeze the lemon juice into storage container, straining out seeds. Set aside.

4. Add remaining water, sugar, honey, peaches, and nutmeg to saucepot. Bring to a boil over medium heat. Reduce heat and simmer uncovered for 20 minutes.

5. Transfer to the bowl of a blender or food processor. Pulse mixture 15–20 times, taking great care to keep the lid on your blender or food processor (the steam from the hot liquid may cause the top to come off). Then process on high until smooth, about 1 minute.

6. Transfer to a storage container and cool to room temperature, about 1 hour. Stir in reserved lemon juice. Chill until completely cold, about 4 hours.

7. To make soda, add 1 cup syrup to each quart of chilled carbonated water. Stir well.

Watermelon Soda

This soda is a riff on the traditional Mexican agua fresca, which translates into "fresh water." In Mexico, chunks of watermelon are crushed by hand and mixed with a little lime juice, sugar, and water. It's served icy cold, so drinking one brings relief on the hottest day. Here, you'll make an agua fresca base in your blender, and then add sparkling water to create a cold, refreshing watermelon soda. The substitution of agave nectar (a sweetener derived from the plant that makes tequila) adds to the Mexican flair.

MAKES 1 QUART BASE, ENOUGH TO MAKE 2 QUARTS SODA

2 quarts water

8 cups watermelon, seeded and cut into 2" cubes

¼ cup light blue agave nectar

Juice of 2 limes

1. Carbonate 2 quarts water with your soda maker, following the manufacturer's directions. Chill on ice or in the refrigerator until cold, about 20 minutes on ice or 1 hour in the fridge.

2. Place watermelon, agave, and lime juice in the bowl of a blender or food processor. Process on high until smooth, about 2 minutes.

3. To make soda, mix equal parts watermelon base and chilled carbonated water. Stir well.

Kiwi Soda

If your kids are craving a store-bought bubble gum soda, give them a kiwi soda instead. With a sweetness that's reminiscent of bubble gum, plus the crunch of kiwi seeds, your family will be delighted by the switch-up. And you'll be delighted by the reduction in sugar, plus the vitamins and fiber contained in this surprising concoction.

MAKES 1 CUP SYRUP, ENOUGH TO FLAVOR 1 QUART CARBONATED WATER

1 quart water
4 kiwis, peeled and coarsely chopped
2 tablespoons simple syrup (equal parts sugar and water)
Juice of ½ lime

1. Carbonate 1 quart water with your soda maker, following the manufacturer's directions. Chill on ice or in the refrigerator until cold, about 20 minutes on ice or 1 hour in the fridge.

2. Place kiwis, simple syrup, and lime juice in the bowl of a blender or food processor. Process on high until smooth, about 2 minutes. Transfer to a storage container and chill until completely cold, about 4 hours.

3. To make soda, place ¼ cup kiwi base into a glass. Add 1 cup chilled carbonated water. Stir gently. Add ice, if desired, and serve.

Seedy Soda?

Depending on the horsepower and speed of your blender or food processor, and the amount of time you purée, you might end up with some seed particles in your base. If you find this soda has too many seeds, simply strain the base through a fine-mesh sieve after you purée it.

Kiwi-Apple Soda

A fruit soda actually made with fruit seems like a blast from the past. Today's fruit-flavored soda, like orange soda or fruit punch, has zero fruit. This fruit soda is mostly fruit and still fizzy.

MAKES 1 CUP SYRUP, ENOUGH TO FLAVOR 1 QUART OR 1 LITER CARBONATED WATER

1 quart water

2 red apples, cored and roughly chopped

3 kiwis, peeled

1. Carbonate 1 quart water with your soda maker, following the manufacturer's directions. Chill on ice or in the refrigerator until cold, about 20 minutes on ice or 1 hour in the fridge.

2. Juice apples and kiwis using a juicer. (If you don't have a juicer, see the sidebar that accompanies Orange Ginger Ale in Chapter 6.) Place in a storage container and cool in refrigerator until completely chilled, about 4 hours.

3. To make soda, place ¼ cup base into a glass. Add 1 cup chilled carbonated water. Stir gently. Add ice, if desired, and serve.

Party Drink Ideas

Change any fruit juice into a party drink with the simple addition of sparkling water. Add fun touches to the kids' cups, such as mini drink umbrellas, swirled paper straws, strawberries suspended in ice cubes, frozen cherries, sliced lemons, star fruit on the end of a skewer, or even a scoop of ice cream in the glass. Use markers and stickers to decorate white paper, wrap the decorative paper around each cup, and add each child's name.

Pineapple Soda

Working with tropical fruit, such as pineapple, can be a little tricky. In their raw form, pineapples contain a good number of strong enzymes, which break down whatever they touch. (This is the reason you can't add fresh pineapple to gelatin and expect it to harden properly.) However, cooking pineapple thoroughly will tame pineapple's nature, while bringing out its inherent sweetness. If you don't want to use fresh pineapple in this soda, canned pineapple will work well, too.

**MAKES 2 CUPS SYRUP, ENOUGH TO FLAVOR 1 QUART
OR 1 LITER CARBONATED WATER**

1 quart plus 1 cup water, divided

½ cup sugar

¼ cup honey

1 large fresh pineapple, peeled, cored, and coarsely chopped, or 3 cups unsweetened canned pineapple chunks

Pinch sage

Pinch nutmeg

½ teaspoon vanilla

1. Carbonate 1 quart water with your soda maker, following the manufacturer's directions. Chill on ice or in the refrigerator until cold, about 20 minutes on ice or 1 hour in the fridge.

2. Place remaining water, sugar, honey, pineapple, sage, and nutmeg into saucepot. Bring to a boil over medium heat. Reduce heat and simmer uncovered for 20 minutes. Cool to room temperature, about 1 hour. Stir in vanilla.

3. Transfer to the bowl of a blender or food processor. Then process on high until smooth, about 1 minute.

4. Strain through a wire-mesh sieve, pressing on solids with the back of a spoon to extract as much liquid as possible. Transfer to a storage container and chill until completely cold, about 4 hours.

5. To make soda, add ½ cup syrup to a glass. Add 1 cup chilled carbonated water. Stir gently. Add ice, if desired, and serve.

Rhubarb Soda

The arrival of rhubarb in the spring marks the first crop of the year. Along with asparagus and lettuce, rhubarb is ready to enjoy early in the growing season. With a tart flavor, this stalk makes a perfect dry soda. The blush pink color of this drink makes it lovely to serve at a spring bridal or baby shower. Don't worry that the base is a little thicker than other soda bases—it will still carbonate well.

MAKES 1 CUP BASE, ENOUGH TO FLAVOR 1 LITER OR 1 QUART CARBONATED WATER

1 quart plus 1 cup chilled water, divided

2 cups of ½" pieces rhubarb (from roughly 1 pound or 5–6 stalks rhubarb)

¼ cup sugar

2 (½" × 3") strips orange zest, orange part only

1. Carbonate 1 quart water with your soda maker, following the manufacturer's directions. Chill on ice or in the refrigerator until cold, about 20 minutes on ice or 1 hour in the fridge.

2. Place remaining water, rhubarb, sugar, and orange zest into a small, heavy saucepot. Bring to a boil over medium heat. Reduce heat and cook uncovered until rhubarb falls apart easily, about 10–15 minutes.

3. Strain through a wire-mesh sieve, pressing on rhubarb mixture with the back of a wooden spoon to extract as much liquid as possible. Cool at room temperature for 1 hour. Transfer to a storage container and place in refrigerator. Cool until completely chilled, at least 4 hours.

4. To make soda, place ¼ cup rhubarb syrup into the bottom of a glass. Top with 1 cup sparkling water. Stir gently to combine. Add ice, if desired, and serve.

Syrups Without the Strain

You'll notice many of the syrups in this book call for you to cook, purée, and strain fruit in order to create a soda base. That's because pressing the base through a wire-mesh sieve pulls particles out of the syrup, which makes the base easier to carbonate. However, if you have a high-horsepower blender (the kind that can turn flaxseeds into powder, or make peanut butter out of roasted peanuts), you can skip the straining step. Simply purée the fruit base in your blender for an extended period of time, like 4–5 minutes. This will break down the fruit's skin and fiber to the point where it will carbonate well. The only caveat: Make sure you remove fruit pits, whole spices, and strips of citrus zest before you purée. Fruit pits may damage your blender's blades, and whole spices and/or zests will throw off the balance of flavors in your base.

Low-Calorie Rhubarb Soda

Rhubarb, despite claims that it's astringent, actually requires less sweetening than many recipes lead you to believe. Here, you'll make a soda base by simmering rhubarb and orange, adding just 1 tablespoon of sweetener at the end.

MAKES 1 CUP BASE, ENOUGH TO FLAVOR 1 LITER OR 1 QUART CARBONATED WATER

1 quart plus 1 cup chilled water, divided
2 cups ½" pieces rhubarb (from roughly 1 pound or 5–6 stalks rhubarb)
1 orange, cut in half
1 tablespoon stevia

1. Carbonate 1 quart water with your soda maker, following the manufacturer's directions. Chill on ice or in the refrigerator until cold, about 20 minutes on ice or 1 hour in the fridge.

2. Place remaining water, rhubarb, and orange halves into a small, heavy saucepot. Bring to a boil over medium heat. Reduce heat and cook uncovered for 1 hour.

3. Strain through a wire-mesh sieve, pressing on rhubarb mixture with the back of a wooden spoon to extract as much liquid as possible. Stir in stevia. Cool at room temperature for 1 hour.

Transfer to a storage container and place in refrigerator. Cool until completely chilled, at least 4 hours.

4. To make soda, place ¼ cup rhubarb syrup into the bottom of a glass. Top with 1 cup sparkling water. Stir gently to combine. Add ice, if desired, and serve.

Mango Soda

This mango soda is a snap to make because you simply boil down prepared mango nectar, which is available where Latin American and Asian foods are sold. If you'd like to make mango soda from fruit, instead of prepared nectar, follow the recipe for Mango Mint Soda (see Chapter 9) and omit the mint.

MAKES 1 CUP SYRUP, ENOUGH TO FLAVOR 1 QUART OR 1 LITER CARBONATED WATER

1 quart chilled water

4 cups (32 ounces; about 2–3 cans) canned unsweetened mango nectar

Pinch ground cinnamon

Pinch ground nutmeg

1 tablespoon fresh lemon juice

1. Carbonate 1 quart water with your soda maker, following the manufacturer's directions. Chill on ice or in the refrigerator until cold, about 20 minutes on ice or 1 hour in the fridge.

2. Place mango nectar, cinnamon, and nutmeg into a large, heavy saucepot. Bring to a boil over high heat.

3. Reduce heat to medium and simmer uncovered until mixture is reduced by ¾, about 30 minutes.

4. Remove from heat and allow to cool to room temperature, about 1 hour.

5. Stir in lemon juice. Pour syrup into a storage container. Refrigerate until completely chilled, about 4 hours.

6. To make mango soda, place ¼ cup syrup into a glass. Add 1 cup chilled carbonated water and stir gently. Add ice, if desired, and serve.

Buying Mango Nectar

Many grocery stores carry mango nectar in the Latin American or ethnic ingredients aisle. You can find it in cans, glass bottles, or cartons. If your grocer doesn't carry it, take a quick trip to your local Latin American or Asian grocery market. These stores stock loads of different juices and nectars. If your community doesn't have such a store, substitute mango juice that's been blended with orange juice and/or pineapple juice (or other fruit juices).

CHAPTER 9

Herbal and Dry Sodas

While most sodas are inherently sweet (coming from sugar, fruit, and/or noncaloric sweeteners), herbal and dry sodas are a less saccharine change of pace. The recipes in this section use less sugar than in previous chapters, so the true flavor of the other ingredients really shines through. Although this section is targeted to grown-up palates, don't be surprised if your kids like dry sodas, as well!

Cucumber Soda

While it may seem a little odd to make a soft drink out of cucumber, once you try it, you'll be a convert. It's akin to floating cucumber slices in water on a warm day. Only here, it's lightly spiced, sweetened, and touched with a little sparkle. Great served with a wedge of lemon or lime!

**MAKES 1 CUP SYRUP, ENOUGH TO FLAVOR 1 QUART
OR 1 LITER CARBONATED WATER**

1 quart plus ½ cup water, divided

½ cup sugar

Zest of ½ lemon, yellow part only, taken off in long strips with a peeler

Pinch dried rosemary

Pinch dried sage

Pinch dried thyme

1 large English cucumber, peeled, seeded, and cut into large chunks

1. Carbonate 1 quart water with your soda maker, following the manufacturer's directions. Chill on ice or in the refrigerator until cold, about 20 minutes on ice or 1 hour in the fridge.

2. Place remaining water, sugar, lemon zest, rosemary, sage, and thyme into a small, heavy saucepot. Bring to a boil over medium heat. Remove from heat and allow to cool to room temperature, about 30 minutes.

3. Strain syrup into the bowl of a blender or food processor. Add cucumber. Pulse mixture 15–20 times. Then process on high until smooth, about 1 minute.

4. Transfer to a storage container. Chill until completely cold, about 4 hours.

5. To make soda, add 1 cup syrup to each quart of chilled carbonated water. Stir well.

Gardener's Bounty

If you grow cucumbers, you know that they all ripen within a few weeks, leaving you with an abundance of produce to eat all at one time. Cucumbers don't freeze or dehydrate well, and there are only so many pickles you can make. One solution is to make cucumber soda. It's refreshing and different. Plus, the cucumber syrup does freeze well, meaning you can have a taste of your summer harvest all year long.

Lemon Thyme Soda

Lemon and thyme pair so naturally that nature makes a version of it—lemon thyme. Now you can make a carbonated beverage that mimics the lemon thyme plant. Simply make a carbonated lemonade with the addition of a few sprigs of thyme. You'll notice the "green" flavor of the thyme mellows the lemon's acidity.

MAKES 1 CUP SYRUP, ENOUGH TO FLAVOR 1 QUART OR 1 LITER CARBONATED WATER

1 quart plus ½ cup water, divided

3 lemons

½ orange

½ cup sugar

4–6 sprigs fresh thyme

Pinch salt, preferably a natural salt like kosher or sea salt

1. Carbonate 1 quart water with your soda maker, following the manufacturer's directions. Chill on ice or in the refrigerator until cold, about 20 minutes on ice or 1 hour in the fridge.

2. Using a peeler, remove zest from lemons and orange half, ensuring you remove only the colored part and leave the white behind. Place zest into a small saucepot.

3. Juice lemons into a storage container, straining out seeds. Store in refrigerator. Reserve orange half for another use.

4. Add remaining water, sugar, thyme, and salt to pot. Bring mixture to a boil, reduce heat to simmer, and cook uncovered for 20 minutes.

5. Remove from heat and cool for 20 minutes. Strain into storage container.

6. Stir in reserved lemon juice. Cool in refrigerator until completely chilled, about 4 hours.

7. To make soda, place ¼ cup syrup into a glass. Add 1 cup carbonated water. Stir gently. Add ice, if desired, and serve.

Lemongrass Soda

A staple throughout Southeast Asia, lemongrass is used in a variety of soups, stews, and sauces. With a flavor that resembles lemon, but is less sour and slightly floral in taste, lemongrass can also make a delicious beverage. Try making this soda for your next Asian-inspired party. It's terrific on its own, or added to vodka- or sake-based cocktails.

MAKES 1 CUP SYRUP, ENOUGH TO FLAVOR 1 QUART OR 1 LITER CARBONATED WATER

1 quart plus 1 cup water, divided

2 stalks lemongrass

½ cup white sugar

Zest of ½ lemon, peeled off in large strips with a vegetable peeler

½ star anise or ¼ teaspoon whole fennel seeds

1 kaffir lime leaf (optional)

¼ teaspoon ground dried ginger

1 (8" × 16") piece cheesecloth

1. Carbonate 1 quart water with your soda maker, following the manufacturer's directions. Chill on ice or in the refrigerator until cold, about 20 minutes on ice or 1 hour in the fridge.

2. Wash lemongrass stalks. Cut lemongrass 4–5" from the bottom, and discard tops. Slice lemongrass pieces in half lengthwise. Remove tough outer layers of lemongrass and discard. Slice lemongrass into ¼" dice.

3. Place lemongrass into a small, heavy saucepan with sugar, remaining water, lemon zest, anise or fennel, and lime leaf (if using). Bring to a boil over medium heat. Then simmer, uncovered, for 20 minutes.

4. Remove syrup from heat and add ginger. Allow to cool to room temperature, stirring occasionally, about 1 hour.

5. Rinse cheesecloth under cold water. Wring out and fold in half so that you have a square. Line a funnel with cheesecloth. Pour syrup into a storage container through the cheesecloth-lined funnel. Cool in refrigerator until completely chilled, about 4 hours.

6. To make soda, add 1 cup syrup to each quart of chilled carbonated water. Stir well.

Kaffir Lime

This recipe calls for kaffir lime, which is a fruit commonly found in Southeast Asia, in Vietnam, Thailand, Indonesia, the Philippines, India, and Bangladesh. You'll find that some Southeast Asian recipes (like Tom Yum, a piquant Thai soup) call for kaffir lime leaves. They add pleasantly tart flavor to dishes. You can find kaffir leaves either dried or frozen in Asian grocers. Fresh, dried, or frozen leaves work equally well in lemongrass soda. And if you can't find kaffir leaves, the soda is just as good without them.

Mango Mint Soda

This soda is like taking a delicious trip to the Caribbean. Joining sweet mango with the fresh kick of mint, you'll love this soda alongside any tropical foods— from rice and peas to jerk chicken to fish tacos. Make up a little extra of the soda base—it's great when blended with lime juice, ice, and rum for a frozen fruity daiquiri.

MAKES 1 CUP SYRUP, ENOUGH TO FLAVOR 1 QUART OR 1 LITER CARBONATED WATER

1 quart plus 1 cup water, divided

1 lime

½ cup white sugar

3 mangoes, peeled, pitted, and coarsely chopped, or 3 cups frozen mango

10–12 sprigs fresh mint

1. Carbonate 1 quart water with your soda maker, following the manufacturer's directions. Chill on ice or in the refrigerator until cold, about 20 minutes on ice or 1 hour in the fridge.

2. Using a peeler, remove zest from lime, ensuring you remove only the colored part and leave the white behind. Place zest into a medium saucepot.

3. Juice lime into a storage container, straining out seeds. Store in refrigerator.

4. Add remaining water, sugar, mangoes, and mint to the pot with the lime zest. Bring to a boil over medium heat. Then simmer, uncovered, for 20 minutes.

5. Remove syrup from heat. Remove mint sprigs. Allow to cool to room temperature, stirring occasionally, about 1 hour.

6. Transfer to the bowl of a blender or food processor. Process until smooth, about 2 minutes. Pour into a storage container and cool in refrigerator until completely chilled, about 4 hours.

7. To make soda, add 1 cup syrup to each quart of chilled carbonated water. Stir well.

Lime Basil Soda

This soda is bursting with the flavors of sultry Southeast Asia. It's tart with a hint of the licorice sweetness that basil imparts. For an interesting twist, dry some Thai or opal basil and use in place of the dried basil used in this recipe. Regardless of the basil you use, lime basil soda is the perfect pairing with the flavors of Southeast Asian cuisine. This soda is especially delicious with Lemongrass Soda–Brined Pork Chops with Mint-Basil-Cilantro Pesto (see Chapter 12).

MAKES 1 CUP SYRUP, ENOUGH TO FLAVOR 1 QUART CARBONATED WATER

1 quart plus ½ cup water, divided

3 large limes, or 10 small Key limes

½ cup sugar

1 tablespoon dried basil

Pinch salt, preferably a natural salt like kosher or sea salt

Juice of ½ lemon

1. Carbonate 1 quart water with your soda maker, following the manufacturer's directions. Chill on ice or in the refrigerator until cold, about 20 minutes on ice or 1 hour in the fridge.

2. Using a peeler, remove zest from limes, ensuring you remove only the colored part and leave the white behind. Place zest into a small saucepot.

3. Juice limes into a storage container, straining out seeds. Store in refrigerator.

4. Add remaining water, sugar, basil, and salt to pot. Bring mixture to a boil, reduce heat to simmer, and cook uncovered for 20 minutes.

5. Remove from heat and cool for 20 minutes. Strain into storage container.

6. Stir in reserved lime juice and lemon juice. Cool in refrigerator until completely chilled, about 4 hours.

7. To make soda, put ⅓ cup syrup into a glass. Top with 1 cup carbonated water. Gently stir. Add ice, if desired, and serve.

Using Different Basil Varieties

Some of the fun of making your own sodas comes from using atypical varieties of produce. And basil is a prime example of a plant that has many different types. Dried basil, as well as the most common fresh basil, is sweet basil, which tastes herbaceous, a little bit like licorice, and is generally mild in flavor. Other basil varieties have the same basic flavor as sweet basil, but taste more like licorice, grass, or even spice. For example, Thai basil has a more pronounced licorice taste. Opal basil tastes a bit grassier, plus has a hint of anise, and is purple in color. Find these basils at farmers' markets, natural/organic grocers, or ethnic grocers. Or, if you have a sunny plot of land, grow your own!

Grapefruit Sage Soda

Grapefruit and sage have a natural affinity for one another. Each has a slightly bitter, slightly pine-like flavor that, when combined, creates a delicious, refreshing soda. A pinch of rosemary helps to heighten the flavor of each, while not overwhelming either's flavor. This soda is great on its own, or with a touch of berry syrup to add flavor and color.

MAKES 2 CUPS SYRUP, ENOUGH TO FLAVOR 2 QUARTS CARBONATED WATER

2 quarts plus 1 cup water, divided

2 whole grapefruits

1 cup sugar

6 large sprigs fresh sage

Pinch dried rosemary

Juice of ½ lime

1. Carbonate 2 quarts water with your soda maker, following the manufacturer's directions. Chill on ice or in the refrigerator until cold, about 20 minutes on ice or 1 hour in the fridge.

2. Using a peeler, remove zest from grapefruits, ensuring you remove only the colored part and leave the white behind. Place zest into a small saucepot.

3. Juice grapefruits into a storage container, straining out seeds. Store in refrigerator.

4. Add remaining water, sugar, sage, and rosemary to pot. Bring mixture to a boil, reduce heat to simmer, and cook uncovered for 20 minutes.

5. Remove from heat and cool for 20 minutes. Strain into storage container.

6. Stir in reserved grapefruit juice and lime juice. Cool in refrigerator until completely chilled, about 4 hours.

7. To make soda, put ⅓ cup syrup into a glass. Top with 1 cup carbonated water. Gently stir. Add ice, if desired, and serve.

Berry and Citrus: A Natural Pair

This recipe suggests that you add a bit of berry syrup to the finished soda to add a unique twist, and you may wonder which berry syrup tastes best. The truth is that berries and citrus mix and match pretty well, and it's difficult to find a flavor combination that won't work. Try a little blackberry with grapefruit sage soda. Or add a raspberry flavor to lime soda. Mix tart cranberry syrup in with orange soda. You'll find they all taste delicious. The sweetness of the berries will balance the bright acidic flavor in citrus-based sodas.

Hibiscus Soda

With a lovely red color, and the faint flavor of ripe raspberries, hibiscus flowers make a great soda. If you're trying to cut back on sugar without making the switch to another sweetener, hibiscus soda is a perfect option. It's bursting with sweet-tart flavor, but has only 1 tablespoon of sugar per 8-ounce serving. Great on its own, or with a squeeze of citrus.

**MAKES 1 CUP SYRUP, ENOUGH TO FLAVOR 1 QUART
OR 1 LITER CARBONATED WATER**

1 quart plus 1 cup water, divided
¼ cup dried hibiscus flowers
¼ cup sugar

1. Carbonate 1 quart water with your soda maker, following the manufacturer's directions. Chill on ice or in the refrigerator until cold, about 20 minutes on ice or 1 hour in the fridge.

2. Place hibiscus flowers in a small bowl or 2-cup glass measuring cup.

3. Bring remaining water to a boil. Turn off heat and let water cool for 30 seconds.

4. Pour boiled water over hibiscus flowers and stir. Steep, uncovered, for 10 minutes.

5. Drain liquid through a wire-mesh sieve, pressing on the flowers with the back of a spoon to extract as much liquid as possible. Discard flowers, or save to use as a garnish.

6. Stir sugar into hibiscus liquid until it's completely dissolved. Transfer to a storage container and refrigerate until completely chilled, about 4 hours.

7. To make soda, place ¼ cup hibiscus syrup into the bottom of a glass. Top with 1 cup carbonated water and stir gently. Add ice, if desired, and serve.

Substitutions for Hibiscus

If you're having issues finding hibiscus flowers (or you find quantities that are too large for you to buy), head to the coffee and tea aisle of your local grocer. Here, you'll find herbal tea blends that contain hibiscus. (They usually have names with "red" or "zing" in them.) Although there are other ingredients in these teas, the prominent flavor is hibiscus, and the rest of the blend will simply add nuance to your hibiscus soda. These tea blends may be loose, in which case you can substitute an equal measure of tea blend for the hibiscus flowers in this recipe. If you find bagged teas, carefully cut open the tea bags with scissors and pour the contents into a measuring cup. Once you've opened enough tea bags to get ¼ cup of tea blend, use that amount instead of hibiscus in this recipe.

Sorrel Soda

Sorrel is a green herb with a slight flavor of lemon. When it blooms, it has red flowers, which are often confused with hibiscus because of a similar appearance. In this recipe, you'll use sorrel leaves, giving your soda a green color, which is decidedly distinct from the red Hibiscus Soda in this chapter.

MAKES 1 CUP SYRUP, ENOUGH TO FLAVOR 1 QUART CARBONATED WATER

1 quart plus ½ cup chilled water, divided

Pinch dried basil or dried tarragon

¼ cup sugar

¾ cup thinly sliced sorrel leaves

Juice of 1 lime

1. Carbonate 1 quart water with your soda maker, following the manufacturer's directions. Chill on ice or in the refrigerator until cold, about 20 minutes on ice or 1 hour in the fridge.

2. Place basil or tarragon, sugar, and remaining water in a small saucepan. Bring to a boil over medium heat. Remove from heat and let syrup cool completely, about 1 hour.

3. Place sorrel leaves into the bowl of a blender or food processor. Add syrup. Purée until smooth. Pour through a wire-mesh sieve into a storage container, pressing on solids with the back of a spoon to extract as much liquid as possible. Stir in lime juice. Refrigerate until cold, at least 4 hours.

4. To make soda, place ¼ cup sorrel syrup into a glass and add 1 cup chilled carbonated water. Stir gently. Add ice, if desired, and serve.

Pairing Alcohol with Dry and Herbal Sodas

Standard highball drinks—rum and cola, or whiskey and ginger ale—mix alcohol with classic sodas. Pairing alcohol with dry sodas or sodas infused with herbs, however, is a bit more challenging. In general, clear liquors, such as vodka, gin, or white rum, blend nicely with the flavors in these sodas. Vodka, being neutral in taste, is a natural, as it adds just a kick of alcohol without imparting much flavor. White rum also goes nicely, as it's a tropical flavor and many dry or herbal sodas are tropical in nature. Gin is an interesting and unique choice—it's flavored primarily with juniper, a piney-tasting bud, along with a number of other herbs and spices. By mixing gin with herbal or floral soda, you'll bring out some of the other flavors in gin—like rosemary, tarragon, or thyme.

Orange Lavender Soda

While orange soda and lavender soda are tasty on their own, the combination of orange and lavender is heavenly. The sweetness and tang of orange melds with floral lavender in a way that brings out the best in both.

MAKES 1½ CUPS SYRUP, ENOUGH TO FLAVOR 1½ QUARTS
OR 1½ LITERS CARBONATED WATER

1½ quarts plus 1 cup water, divided
1 orange
1 cup sugar
3 tablespoons dried culinary lavender flowers

1. Carbonate 1½ quarts water with your soda maker, following the manufacturer's directions. Chill on ice or in the refrigerator until cold, about 20 minutes on ice or 1 hour in the fridge.

2. Using a peeler, remove zest from orange, taking care to remove as little of the white part as possible, and place into a medium heavy saucepot. Juice orange into a storage container and set aside. Add remaining water, sugar, and lavender to pot with orange zest. Bring to a boil over medium heat. Remove pot from heat and steep uncovered for 10 minutes. Strain syrup through a wire-mesh sieve. Transfer to a storage container and let rest at room temperature until cool, about 1 hour. Add reserved orange juice and place in refrigerator. Chill until completely cold, about 4 hours.

3. To make soda, add ¼ cup syrup to a glass. Top with 1 cup sparkling water and gently stir. Add ice, if desired, and serve.

Matching Herbs with Fruit

Use this chapter as a great jumping-off point for flavor experimentation. The recipes provided here give you flavor combinations that are guaranteed to work well together, and will give you an idea of whether you like herbal sodas. If you do, turn your kitchen into a fruit and herb lab! First smell ripe fruits and fresh herbs together. Combinations that smell good together are likely to also taste good together. Find recipes in this book for standalone fruit sodas, and add a few sprigs of the fresh herb when making the sugar syrup for the base. Be sure to take good notes. If you discover a combination you really like, you'll want to make it again!

Pineapple Cilantro Soda

Pineapple and cilantro are found together in many Mexican and Caribbean recipes, such as salsas and salads. Their flavors pair naturally, and make for a bright, tropical-flavored soda. The addition of coriander seeds, which are seeds of the cilantro plant, heightens the cilantro flavor.

**MAKES 2 CUPS SYRUP, ENOUGH TO FLAVOR 1 QUART
OR 1 LITER CARBONATED WATER**

1 quart plus 1 cup water, divided

½ cup honey

1 large fresh pineapple, peeled, cored, and coarsely chopped,
or 3 cups unsweetened canned pineapple chunks

8–10 sprigs fresh cilantro

2–3 whole coriander seeds (optional)

1. Carbonate 1 quart water with your soda maker, following the manufacturer's directions. Chill on ice or in the refrigerator until cold, about 20 minutes on ice or 1 hour in the fridge.

2. Place remaining water, honey, pineapple, cilantro, and coriander (if using) into a saucepot. Bring to a boil over medium heat. Reduce heat and simmer uncovered for 20 minutes. Remove from heat and cool to room temperature, about 1 hour.

3. Remove cilantro and coriander seeds.

4. Transfer to the bowl of a blender or food processor. Process on high until smooth, about 1 minute.

5. Strain through a wire mesh sieve, pressing on solids with the back of a spoon to remove as much liquid as possible. Transfer to a storage container and chill until completely cold, about 4 hours.

6. To make soda, add ½ cup syrup to a glass. Add 1 cup chilled carbonated water. Stir gently. Add ice, if desired, and serve.

Lavender Soda

In the United States, lavender is used extensively as a fragrance in body scrubs and hand creams, but is often overlooked as an ingredient in foods. Contrast this with Europe, where the delicate flavor of lavender is used in both sweet and savory dishes, and is an integral part of the herb mixture Herbes de Provence. In this mouthwatering soda, you can discover what many parts of the world already know—that lavender is an essential part of any cook's pantry. For a kick, pair this soda with a little gin and a wheel of lemon for a floral cocktail.

MAKES 1 CUP SYRUP, ENOUGH TO FLAVOR 3 QUARTS OR 3 LITERS CARBONATED WATER

3 quarts plus 1 cup water, divided

1 cup sugar

3 tablespoons dried culinary lavender flowers

Zest of ½ lemon, removed in large strips

1. Carbonate 3 quarts water with your soda maker, following the manufacturer's directions. Chill on ice or in the refrigerator until cold, about 20 minutes on ice or 1 hour in the fridge.

2. Combine remaining water, sugar, lavender, and zest in a medium heavy saucepot. Bring to a boil over medium heat. Remove pot from heat and steep uncovered for 10 minutes. Strain syrup into a storage container and place in refrigerator. Chill until completely cold, about 4 hours.

3. To make soda, add 1 tablespoon plus 1 teaspoon syrup to a glass. Top with 1 cup sparkling water and gently stir. Add ice, if desired, and serve.

Culinary Lavender

When you buy lavender, make sure you're buying lavender flowers that are suitable for consumption. Because most lavender is used for scent, rather than for cooking, many processors spray lavender with chemicals to enhance their aroma or preserve the flowers. To avoid these additives, look for lavender that is labeled "culinary" or "cooking" lavender. This is untreated and safe to eat. You are also perfectly safe if you use lavender from your own garden, provided that you have not sprayed or treated the flowers with chemicals.

Part 3

FANTASTIC FOODS AND DELICIOUS DRINKS MADE WITH HOMEMADE SODA

Why stop at simply making drinks with your soda bases? This section provides you with a plethora of ways to incorporate your sparkly beverages into other recipes. From nonalcoholic drinks and cocktails, to entrées, side dishes, and desserts, you may find yourself making homemade soft drinks simply to put into other dishes and drinks!

CHAPTER 10

Mocktails

Now that you have a supply of homemade sodas, you can craft artisanal nonalcoholic drinks (also called "mocktails") quickly. Your own soda will add artistic flair and intense flavor to otherwise humdrum beverages. No one will miss the alcohol in these yummy concoctions!

Classic Root Beer Float

What complements the flavor of your own homemade root beer better than homemade vanilla ice cream? The mellow vanilla and cream are the perfect foil for the spiciness of root beer. This classic is both a drink and a dessert, making it the perfect end to any meal. And if you don't have time to (or don't choose to) make ice cream, feel free to substitute any high-quality vanilla ice cream.

SERVES 4

2 cups half and half

1 vanilla bean, split lengthwise and scraped

⅔ cup sugar

6 egg yolks

2 cups heavy cream

4 cups Root Beer (see Chapter 5)

1. Combine half and half, vanilla bean, and vanilla seeds in a medium saucepan. Bring to a simmer; then remove from heat, cover, and let steep for 20 minutes.

2. Beat together sugar and egg yolks with a mixer until very thick and pale yellow, about 4 minutes.

3. Remove vanilla bean from saucepan and bring back to a simmer. While beating egg mixture, slowly add half of hot half and half. Return mixture to the saucepan with the remaining half and half, and cook over medium heat, stirring constantly until mixture thickens, about 5–7 minutes.

4. Strain mixture through a wire-mesh strainer into a bowl that's set over a second bowl filled with ice water. Add cream and stir the mixture until it reaches room temperature, about 10 minutes. Cover and refrigerate for 2 hours.

5. Transfer to an ice-cream maker and freeze according to the manufacturer's instructions. Transfer to a freezer-safe container and freeze until hardened, about 2 hours.

6. Place a scoop of ice cream into the bottom of four beer mugs. Top each with a cup of Root Beer and serve.

Sparkling Iced Tea with Lemon-Mint Honey

Why bother carbonating iced tea? Carbonation brings out the subtleties in the varietal of tea you use and makes for a more dramatic version. Here, you will cold-brew tea. In contrast to adding hot or boiling water to loose tea, cold-brewing preserves the essential oils in the tea leaves (hot water destroys these oils). This tea recipe also features a bonus—tea ice cubes, which keep your sparkling iced tea cold without watering down its flavor.

SERVES 12

1 (8" × 16") piece cheesecloth

1 cup loose black tea, such as Assam, Darjeeling, or Ceylon

10½ cups cold water, divided

1 lemon

1 cup honey

1 tablespoon fresh mint leaves, or 1 teaspoon dried mint leaves

1. Rinse cheesecloth under cold water. Wring out and fold in half so that you have a square. Place tea into center of cheesecloth. Gather corners and edges together to create a pouch and secure with kitchen twine or a rubber band. Place into a large, nonreactive bowl, pot, or pitcher. Add 5 cups water and push tea pouch into water until completely submerged. Cover and let stand for 18–24 hours.

2. While tea brews, make lemon-mint honey. Wash lemon well and slice into ¼" slices. Place into a small saucepan with honey and mint. Bring to a simmer over medium heat. Remove from heat and let steep uncovered until room temperature, about 1 hour. Strain honey into a storage container and refrigerate until ready to use.

3. Remove tea pouch from water and squeeze to extract as much liquid from pouch as possible. You should have about 4–4½ cups of tea concentrate. Discard tea leaves. (Cheesecloth can be used again once you wash it.)

4. Remove ½ cup of tea concentrate and mix with 1½ cups water. Pour into an ice cube tray and freeze until solid, about 6 hours.

5. Carbonate 1 quart water with your soda maker, following the manufacturer's directions. Chill on ice or in the refrigerator until cold, about 20 minutes on ice or 1 hour in the fridge.

6. To make sparkling iced tea, place 2 tea ice cubes into a tall glass. Add 1 cup tea concentrate and 1 cup chilled carbonated water. If desired, add lemon-mint honey to taste. Stir well.

Strawberry-Rhubarb Sparkler

This mocktail is like drinking spring in a glass. The first crops home gardeners, as well as farmers, are able to harvest are often strawberries and rhubarb. Add just a touch of thyme (also available in spring) to the mixture to round out the flavors and add a dash of sophistication.

SERVES 1

5 whole strawberries, divided

1 sprig fresh thyme

1–2 teaspoons sugar

1 cup Rhubarb Soda (see Chapter 8)

½ cup ice

1. Wash strawberries. Stem and coarsely chop four strawberries, saving the last for a garnish.

2. Place strawberries into the bottom of a sturdy glass. Add thyme sprig and 1 teaspoon sugar. Muddle together until well mixed, about 1 minute. Taste for sweetness, adding more sugar if desired. Remove stem and large pieces of thyme from the mixture, leaving muddled leaves with strawberry mixture.

3. Add Rhubarb Soda and stir gently. Add ice. Slice remaining strawberry from the tip toward the stem, leaving the stem and ¼" of the fruit intact. Place on rim of glass as a garnish.

Smooth or Chunky Drinks?

In this recipe, you muddle the strawberries in a glass and top with soda, without straining the strawberries first. This results in a coarse, nearly chewy drink, with lovely bits of strawberries floating in the glass. If you prefer a smoother drink, simply purée the strawberry with sugar in a blender until smooth. Then pour into the glass and top with Rhubarb Soda. As for the thyme? Bend the sprig in half, rub it around the rim of the glass, and either discard or use as a garnish. You don't want to blend the herb with the strawberries, as it would add too much thyme flavor and throw off the balance of the drink.

Lime-Grapefruit Chiller with Mint

This tasty beverage is a nonalcoholic twist on a mojito. You start by muddling fresh mint with sugar and lime, just as you would with a mojito. However, instead of adding rum and soda water, you'll top it with homemade grapefruit soda. The result is delicious and refreshing. If you use pink or red grapefruit to make your soda, this drink takes on a pretty pink blush, making it perfect to serve at a baby shower.

SERVES 1

3 sprigs fresh mint, divided

½ lime

1 tablespoon sugar

½ cup ice

1 cup Grapefruit Soda (see Chapter 6)

1. Remove leaves from 2 sprigs of mint and transfer to a double old-fashioned glass. Slice a ¼"-thick wheel off lime half and set aside. Coarsely chop remaining lime and place into glass with mint.

2. Add sugar and muddle until mint is crushed and lime releases its juices, about 2–3 minutes.

3. Add ice. Top with Grapefruit Soda. Garnish with reserved mint sprig and reserved lime wheel.

Shirley Temple/Roy Rogers

The drink your parents let you order at restaurants gets an upgrade here! Instead of store-bought soda and a splash of maraschino cherry juice or grenadine, you'll use homemade soda and homemade grenadine. (Of course, you are free to substitute store-bought versions of either in a pinch.) To make a Shirley Temple, you'll use lemon-lime soda. To make a Roy Rogers, use cola.

SERVES 1

1 tablespoon unsweetened pomegranate juice

1 tablespoon sugar

2 drops orange or lemon extract, or orange flower water

1 cup Lemon-Lime Soda or Cola (both in Chapter 5; do not use Cherry Cola or Vanilla Cola)

½ cup ice

2–3 maraschino cherries, preferably homemade or artisanal

1. Make grenadine: Place pomegranate juice into a microwave-safe coffee mug and heat 15–30 seconds, until hot, but not boiling. Stir in sugar and extract and cool to room temperature, about 3 minutes.

2. Transfer pomegranate mixture to the bottom of a tall glass. Top with soda and stir gently. Add ice and garnish with cherries.

Making Homemade Grenadine

The combination of pomegranate juice, sugar, and citrus is known as "grenadine." And if you find yourself preparing Shirley Temples or Roy Rogers often (or for a crowd), you can make grenadine in a batch instead of 1 tablespoon at a time. Place 1 cup unsweetened pomegranate juice into a small saucepot. Bring just to a simmer and remove from heat. Add 1 cup sugar and ¼ teaspoon orange or lemon extract, or orange flower water, and stir. Cool to room temperature. Transfer to a container with a tight lid and store in the refrigerator. Stays fresh for 1 month. To use in this recipe, add 1 tablespoon from the batch of homemade grenadine for every 1 cup of homemade soda.

Homemade Maraschino Cherries

We all know them—and some of us love them—the bright red, super-sweet cherries that resemble candy more than they do fruit. But what are maraschino cherries, and can you make them at home? Maraschino cherries are a cherry varietal that grows in Croatia and Italy. The Italians made a liqueur from them, but the cherries themselves became a hit as a cocktail garnish. Commercially prepared maraschino cherries are soaked in salt water, which preserves the flavor, but removes the color. The brined cherries are then soaked in sugar syrup, and dyed their characteristic red. Nowadays, artisanal manufacturers make cherries that use the same process but without harsh chemicals and dyes. Seek these at natural food markets or upscale liquor stores. Or, make your own cherries. Follow the directions for the Cherry Soda in Chapter 7, but chill the cherries in the sugar syrup instead of pressing them through a wire sieve.

Brunswick Cooler

Light and refreshing with a luscious, full body, the Brunswick Cooler is a wonderful celebratory nonalcoholic drink. This recipe calls for making both ginger simple syrup and coriander simple syrup so that you have the flexibility to add the leftover syrups separately to other recipes. However, if you find that you drink Brunswick Coolers frequently, or would like to make a batch for a party, you can make ginger-coriander syrup.

SERVES 1

1 tablespoon granulated sugar

½ teaspoon ground dried ginger

1 tablespoon lemon juice

1 teaspoon Ginger Simple Syrup (recipe follows)

½ teaspoon Coriander Simple Syrup (recipe follows)

¼ cup lemon sherbet or sorbet

1 cup homemade club soda

1 cup ice

1. Prepare rim of a collins glass for the drink: Mix sugar and ginger together and place onto a small saucer. Place lemon juice into a second small saucer. Place glass upside down into saucer of lemon juice, dampening rim of glass. Shake off excess lemon juice. Roll dampened rim of glass in sugar mixture.

2. Pour remaining lemon juice into glass. Add both simple syrups and stir to combine.

3. Add lemon sherbet and club soda. Stir to combine. Add ice to fill glass and serve.

Ginger Simple Syrup

1 (2") piece fresh ginger, peeled and sliced into ¼" slices
½ cup sugar
½ cup water

Combine all ingredients in a microwave-safe measuring cup or bowl. Place in microwave and bring to a boil using high power, about 2–3 minutes. Remove from microwave and leave at room temperature to cool, about 40 minutes. Strain into storage container. Store in the refrigerator.

Coriander Simple Syrup

1 tablespoon whole coriander seeds
½ cup water
½ cup sugar

Heat coriander seeds in a small saucepan over medium heat and cook, stirring constantly, until fragrant, about 30 seconds to 1 minute. Remove from heat and immediately add water and sugar. Return pot to stove and bring to a boil over high heat. Remove from heat and leave at room temperature to cool, about 40 minutes. Strain into storage container. Store in the refrigerator.

Ginger-Coriander Syrup

1 tablespoon whole coriander seeds
1 (2") piece fresh ginger, peeled and sliced into ¼" slices
½ cup water
½ cup sugar

Heat coriander seeds in a small saucepan over medium heat and cook, stirring constantly, until fragrant, about 30 seconds to 1 minute. Remove from heat and immediately add ginger, water, and sugar. Return pot to stove and bring to a boil over high heat. Remove from heat and leave at room temperature to cool, about 40 minutes. Strain into storage container. Store in the refrigerator.

Raspberry Spritzer

A raspberry spritzer is closely related to any of the berry sodas in this cookbook. The major difference is that instead of cooking a simple syrup and adding the juice of the berries, you simply smash the ingredients together and top with soda water. This way, you get the seeds and pulp of the berries for a more rustic take on fruit soda. Feel free to experiment with different fruit in place of the raspberries—any berry will work, as will most stone fruit.

SERVES 1

½ cup fresh or frozen red raspberries (thaw if frozen)

1 tablespoon sugar

1 tablespoon fresh lemon juice

½ cup ice

1 cup homemade club soda

1 lemon twist

1. Place raspberries, sugar, and lemon juice into the bottom of a double old-fashioned glass. Muddle until berries release their juice and sugar is no longer grainy, about 3 minutes. If you desire a drink without raspberry bits, strain mixture through a wire-mesh sieve.

2. Top with ice and soda. Rub lemon twist around the rim of the glass, add lemon twist to drink, and serve.

Lemon Twists

To make a lemon twist, you can use a channel knife or a sharp vegetable peeler. Remove a long strip of lemon peel, taking care to remove only the yellow part and leave the white behind. If you use a peeler, trim the lemon twist into a strip about ¼" wide. Taking great care not to rip the zest, tie the strip of lemon into a knot. This releases the essential oils, which impart a great flavor into the drink.

Virgin Lime Rickey

Supposedly named for a politician, the "rickey" is a simple and classic drink that combines half a lime, a little gin (or rum or vodka), and a healthy topping of soda water. Here, it gets an alcohol-free makeover, which channels the flavor of the cocktail without the boozy punch.

SERVES 1

½ lime, cut into wedges, plus 1 wheel of lime for a garnish

3–4 dashes bitters

1 teaspoon sugar

1½ cups Lime Soda (see Chapter 6)

½ cup ice

1. Place the lime wedges (reserving lime wheel for garnish) in the bottom of a sturdy glass. Add bitters and sugar. Muddle until lime is well broken down and releases its juice, about 1 minute.

2. Top with Lime Soda and stir gently. Add ice, garnish with lime wheel, and serve.

Variation Using Sparkling Water

If you don't have Lime Soda on hand, simply substitute plain club soda and increase the amount of fresh lime and sugar you use: Cut a whole lime into wedges, reserving one wedge as a garnish. Smash the lime with 1 tablespoon sugar into the bottom of a glass, along with 3–4 dashes bitters. Top with 1½ cups soda water, ½ cup ice, and garnish with the reserved lime wedge.

Bubbling Halloween Punch

Both adults and children will be fascinated with this cauldron of orange punch, accented with floating black blobs of ice cream. There are two secrets to keeping this punch fresh-looking for an extended amount of time: First, make ice-cream balls and freeze them on a cookie sheet so they are frozen solid. And second, keep the punch exceptionally well chilled with a spooky ice ring. This ice is kissed with a hint of orange, and barely dilutes the punch as it melts.

SERVES 8–10

1 quart premium dark chocolate ice cream (or make your own—see sidebar)
½ cup orange syrup from the Orange Soda recipe (see Chapter 6)
1 quart water, chilled
2 oranges, cut into thin slices
2 handfuls black plastic spiders, or other small Halloween-themed plastic toys (optional)
2 liters or quarts Orange Soda (see Chapter 6)

1. Make ice-cream balls: Using a ½-cup ice-cream scoop, portion out eight ice-cream balls. Space evenly on a rimmed sheet pan and return to freezer. Freeze until completely solid, overnight or up to 24 hours. (After 24 hours, wrap ice-cream balls and sheet pan in a double layer of plastic. This will keep other smells from the freezer from impacting the taste of the ice cream.)

2. Make ice ring: Mix orange syrup with water. Arrange orange slices inside a ring mold, Bundt pan, or angel food cake pan. If using plastic spiders and/or toys, wash them in warm, soapy water and rinse thoroughly; then give a second rinse in cold water. Arrange around orange slices. Pour orange-water mixture over top. Place in freezer and chill until solid, overnight or up to 24 hours. (After 24 hours, wrap in a double layer of plastic.)

3. To serve, unmold ice ring into a large bowl (or punch bowl). Add chocolate ice cream balls. Carefully pour Orange Soda around, taking care not to lose too much carbonation. Serve immediately.

Homemade Chocolate Ice Cream

If you have time, this recipe is amazingly delicious when you make your own ice cream. Either follow your favorite recipe for dark chocolate ice cream, or modify the steps for making vanilla ice cream (as found in the Classic Root Beer Float recipe in this chapter) as such: Replace the vanilla bean with ½ teaspoon vanilla extract. After cooking the egg mixture until it's thick, add 6 ounces of melted dark chocolate (60 percent cacao or higher), plus ½ cup unsweetened cocoa powder. Finish recipe as written.

Rosemary-Peach Spritzer

Delightful any time of the year, this drink combines the summery flavors of peach and fresh herbs with cranberry, a flavor typically enjoyed during the holidays. The herbaceous flavor of rosemary in this spritzer mimics the flavor of gin in a cocktail with alcohol, making it a great choice for times when you'd like to have a cocktail, but are abstaining from alcohol.

SERVES 1

2 rosemary sprigs (4–6 inches long, each), divided

1 tablespoon fresh lemon juice

2 cups ice cubes, divided

2 tablespoons cranberry juice

1 teaspoon lemon zest

1 tablespoon simple syrup

¼ cup chilled Peach Soda (see Chapter 8)

1 fresh peach slice for garnish (optional)

Pinch nutmeg, or 1 grind nutmeg from a nutmeg grinder

1. Remove leaves from 1 sprig rosemary and place into the bottom of a cocktail shaker with lemon juice. Using a muddler, crush rosemary and juice together.

2. Add 1 cup ice cubes to cocktail shaker. Add cranberry juice, lemon zest, and simple syrup.

3. Shake well to combine, about 20–30 seconds.

4. Place remaining ice into a double old-fashioned glass. Strain rosemary mixture over ice. Top with Peach Soda and stir until mixed.

5. Garnish with remaining rosemary sprig and peach slice, if using. Sprinkle or grind nutmeg over drink.

No-Boil Simple Syrup

Simple syrup is made by boiling equal parts of sugar and water together, so that the sugar dissolves completely, leaving a clear liquid you can use to flavor drinks. However, you can also make simple syrup without boiling—it just takes longer for the sugar to dissolve. To make no-cook simple syrup, mix equal parts white sugar and water in a container. Stir or shake to combine and place into your refrigerator. After 4–6 hours, the sugar has completely dissolved, leaving you with simple syrup.

Piña Colada Slush

Piña coladas harness the flavors of the tropics. Combining creamy coconut with tart pineapple and crushed ice, these drinks have been cooling down vacationers for decades. When you have homemade pineapple soda on hand, you're never very far from these icy delights. And if you'd like to make these mocktails into cocktails, either add 1 cup light rum to the blender with the coconut and pineapple, or float dark rum onto the top of each glass.

SERVES 4

¼ cup flaked coconut

1½ cups ice

1 (15-ounce) can cream of coconut, such as Coco Lopez or Goya

4 cups Pineapple Soda (see Chapter 8), divided

4 fresh pineapple spears or pineapple rings

1. Place coconut into a small pan and heat over medium-high heat, stirring constantly. Toast until golden brown, about 2 minutes. Immediately transfer to a plate and set aside.

2. Place ice, cream of coconut, and 1½ cups Pineapple Soda into the pitcher of a blender. Pulse 15–20 times, breaking up ice. Then blend until smooth, about 1 minute.

3. Divide mixture evenly across four large wine glasses. Top each with equal parts Pineapple Soda. Garnish each with a pineapple spear and a sprinkling of the toasted coconut.

In the Pink Sparkling Lemonade

Lemon soda gets a rosy upgrade with the addition of raspberries and a little cranberry juice. Make this recipe as a change of pace when you tire of simple lemon soda.

SERVES 1

1 slice lemon

2 tablespoons sugar

½ cup fresh or frozen raspberries, divided (thaw if frozen)

2 tablespoons cranberry juice

1 cup chilled Lemon Soda (see Chapter 6)

½ cup ice

1. Run lemon slice across the rim of a tall collins glass. Roll rim of glass in sugar to coat. Save lemon slice to use as a garnish.

2. Wash raspberries, setting two aside for garnish. Place remaining raspberries into the bottom of the glass, along with cranberry juice. Using a muddler, crush the berries and juice together.

3. Top with Lemon Soda, and stir gently until mixed. Add ice and garnish with reserved raspberries and lemon slice.

Vanilla Ice Cream Soda

Root beer isn't the only soda that pairs with vanilla ice cream. In this classic soda shop recipe, you'll make a vanilla soda from vanilla simple syrup and your home-carbonated water, and top with rich vanilla ice cream for an icy treat.

SERVES 1

2 tablespoons water

2 tablespoons sugar

½ teaspoon vanilla extract

1 cup chilled homemade club soda

½ cup high-quality vanilla ice cream (or make your own, following the instructions in the Classic Root Beer Float recipe in this chapter)

Optional garnishes: whipped cream, maraschino cherries, rolled wafer cookie

1. Stir water and sugar together in a microwave-safe container. Heat on high until mixture boils and becomes clear, about 1 minute. Let cool to room temperature and stir in vanilla.

2. Transfer vanilla syrup to the bottom of a tall collins glass or mug. Add club soda and stir. Top with ice cream and garnish with whipped cream, cherries, and/or cookie, if desired.

Making a Batch of Vanilla Syrup

Having vanilla syrup on hand makes it simple to put together vanilla ice cream sodas any time you like, and also is great for adding a flavor of vanilla to other beverages, such as colas or coffee drinks. To make a 1-cup batch of vanilla syrup, split a vanilla bean in half lengthwise, scraping the seeds into a small, heavy saucepot. Add scraped pods, along with 1 cup water and 1 cup sugar, to pot. Bring to a boil over medium heat. Remove from heat and let cool to room temperature, about 1 hour. Transfer syrup to a storage container and store in your refrigerator for up to 1 month. You may leave the vanilla pods in the syrup or remove them. If you leave them in, the syrup's vanilla flavor will become more intense over time.

CHAPTER 11

Cocktails

Cocktails—both traditional and contemporary—benefit from a hint of sparkle. The effervescence cleanses your palate, enabling you to taste more intricate flavors. Cocktail trends are calling for fresh, artisanal ingredients, like small-batch, natural, and homemade sodas. By using your home-crafted soft drinks in cocktails, it's like having a professional bartender running your home bar.

Moscow Mule

A Moscow Mule delights the pickiest palate. With spice from your homemade ginger ale, the pleasant tang of lime, and a little kick (that's what makes it a mule) of vodka, this drink is nicely balanced. Moscow Mules are traditionally served in iced copper mugs, however you may serve them in any well-chilled drinkware.

SERVES 1

2 sprigs fresh mint, divided

1 teaspoon Ginger Simple Syrup (see Chapter 10)

Juice of ½ lime

2 tablespoons plain vodka

½ cup cubed ice

½ cup Ginger Ale (see Chapter 5)

1. Remove leaves from 1 sprig of mint, reserving the second sprig as a garnish. Place leaves into the bottom of a chilled mug and add Ginger Simple Syrup. Muddle together.

2. Add lime juice and vodka. Stir well.

3. Add ice and top with Ginger Ale. Garnish with reserved mint sprig and serve.

Old-Fashioned

The Old-Fashioned is so named because it's believed to be one of the oldest American cocktails. That explains why it's also considered a classic cocktail! Although you can make this drink with any of a number of liquors, brown spirits are the most common. In the South, it's traditional to use bourbon or rye whiskey, whereas in the state of Wisconsin, you'll find brandy to be the most common liquor used. All are delicious!

SERVES 1

2 (¼"-thick) slices orange, divided
2 maraschino cherries, divided
5 drops Angostura bitters
¼ cup bourbon, brandy, rye, Southern Comfort, or whiskey
¼ cup homemade club soda
½ cup ice

1. Place 1 slice orange and 1 cherry into the bottom of a double old-fashioned glass and add bitters. Muddle together into a fine paste, about 30 seconds.

2. Add alcohol and club soda. Stir well.

3. Add ice, garnish with reserved orange slice and cherry, and serve.

Out of Fruit?

If you lack the requisite orange and/or cherry for this drink, you can still make a delicious cocktail. Substitute sugar for the fruit. In the first step, simply stir 1 teaspoon of granulated white sugar with the bitters. Then proceed with the recipe as written. Garnish with a lemon twist and enjoy.

Dark and Stormy

The origins of this drink hail from Bermuda, where Gosling's Black Seal Rum (from Bermuda) is topped with fresh lime and ginger beer. The recipe published here requires you to take a few liberties with the original recipe. First off, you'll use your own ginger ale, rather than a ginger beer. (Ginger beer is fermented, which provides the carbonation, whereas homemade ginger ale is a combination of ginger simple syrup and club soda.) In addition, this recipe doesn't require you to hunt down Gosling's Black Seal Rum. Any dark rum will do. And if you're feeling spicy, substitute a spiced dark rum.

SERVES 1

½ lime

1 teaspoon Ginger Simple Syrup (see Chapter 10)

2 ounces dark rum

½ cup ice

½ cup Ginger Ale (see Chapter 5)

1. Cut a wedge from the lime half and set aside. Squeeze remaining lime half into a tall collins glass.

2. Add Ginger Simple Syrup and rum. Mix well. Add ice.

3. Top with Ginger Ale. Garnish with reserved lime wedge and serve.

Pimm's Cup

Pimm's is a botanical liqueur based on gin, with a proprietary blend of fruits, herbs, and spices infused into it. Created in a bar in England during the nineteenth century, Pimm's is a popular British drink. When skillfully combined with cucumber, lemon, and your own homemade soda, the result is a Pimm's Cup, a traditional summer cocktail.

SERVES 1

¼ lemon

1 (½") slice cucumber, peeled and seeded

1 teaspoon Ginger Simple Syrup (see Chapter 10)

¼ cup Pimm's No. 1

½ cup ice

½ cup Lemon-Lime Soda (see Chapter 5) or Ginger Ale (see Chapter 5),
or—for a real twist—Lemon Thyme Soda (see Chapter 9)

2 sprigs fresh thyme

1. Using a channel knife (preferred) or a sharp vegetable peeler, remove a long strip of lemon peel, taking care to remove only the yellow part and leave the white behind. (If you use a peeler, next trim the lemon zest into a strip about ¼" wide.) Taking great care not to rip the zest, tie the strip of lemon into a knot. Set aside.

2. Place remaining lemon, cucumber, and Ginger Simple Syrup into a double old-fashioned glass. Muddle together until lemon has released its juice and cucumber is broken down, about 2 minutes.

3. Add Pimm's and ice. Top with your preference of homemade soda, and garnish with reserved lemon twist and thyme sprigs.

Sparkling Pomegranate Sake-tini

Sake, a brewed rice beverage from Japan, makes lovely cocktails. It has a neutral flavor, making it great for blending. In addition, the alcohol content of sake is roughly the same as wine (about 15 percent), so using it in cocktails with nonalcoholic mixers allows you to keep your wits about you. Higher-quality sake is made from rice with more of the bran removed, a process known as polishing. For this recipe, you'll want to use a high-quality sake rice that's been polished more than 40 percent.

SERVES 1–2, DEPENDING ON THE SIZE OF YOUR GLASSES

½ cup unflavored sake, preferably more than 40 percent polished

1 tablespoon Ginger Simple Syrup (see Chapter 10)

½ cup ice

½ cup Sparkling Pomegranate Soda (see Chapter 7)

8–10 pomegranate seeds

1. Place sake, Ginger Simple Syrup, and ice together into a cocktail shaker. Shake until well blended and icy, about 1 minute.

2. Strain into a large martini glass, or strain into 2 small martini glasses, dividing equally. Top with Sparkling Pomegranate. Float pomegranate seeds on top of cocktail. Serve.

Effervescent Margarita

Margaritas are usually shaken over ice, or blended with ice to form a slushy, frozen drink. Now you can add a new version of this Mexican drink to your repertoire—a carbonated margarita. Your homemade lime soda is the perfect foil to tequila, lime juice, and orange liqueur.

SERVES 1–2, DEPENDING ON THE SIZE OF YOUR GLASSES

½ lime

¼ cup salt, preferably a natural salt like kosher or sea salt

3 tablespoons 100 percent agave tequila

1 tablespoon orange liqueur, such as Cointreau or triple sec

½ cup ice

½ cup Lime Soda (see Chapter 6)

1. Run lime around the rim of a large martini glass (or two small martini glasses). Roll in salt to create a salted rim and set aside.

2. Squeeze lime into a cocktail shaker and drop juiced lime into shaker. Add tequila, orange liqueur, and ice. Cover shaker and shake vigorously for 45–60 seconds. Strain mixture into prepared glass(es). Top with Lime Soda and serve.

Flavored Margaritas

While you think you wouldn't tire of a plain margarita, there are times you want to mix things up. Or, you may crave a sparkling margarita, but lack lime soda. Not to fret—you can make this recipe with other fruit sodas. Simply substitute an equal amount of another fruit soda for the lime soda here. You'll also want to change the salt rim. While salt is fine for lime and other sour citrus fruits (like lemon or grapefruit), swap in a sugar rim for other flavors. Replace an equal amount of sugar for the salt in this recipe.

Lemon-Gin Sparkling Cocktail

This drink is a variation on a French 75, which is a cocktail made with gin, lemon juice, and champagne. The basis of this lemon-gin sparkling cocktail is still gin, but instead of champagne, you'll use lemon soda plus coriander simple syrup. The simple syrup intensifies the flavor of the gin, as coriander is usually one of the spices in gin. The addition of a rosemary sprig also brings out the flavor of the gin. If you want a real change-up, use fresh cilantro as a garnish instead of rosemary.

SERVES 1

2 sprigs fresh rosemary (4–6 inches each), divided (may substitute cilantro)

1 tablespoon lemon juice

1 teaspoon Coriander Simple Syrup (see Chapter 10)

¼ cup gin

1 cup ice, divided

1 cup Lemon Soda (see Chapter 6)

1. Remove leaves from one sprig of rosemary and place into the bottom of a cocktail with lemon juice and Coriander Simple Syrup. Muddle until rosemary is well broken down, about 1 minute.

2. Add gin and ½ cup ice and shake to combine, about 1 minute.

3. Strain into a tall collins glass. Add remaining ice. Top with Lemon Soda. Garnish with remaining rosemary and serve.

Eastside Fizz

This cool and refreshing cocktail is the perfect answer to a hot day. The herbal punch from the gin, cucumber, and mint is balanced with a hint of sugar, and brought together with a little effervescence. This drink usually calls for club soda or tonic water. Here, you upgrade the cocktail by making it with your homemade cucumber soda.

SERVES 1

1 (4") section English cucumber

2 sprigs mint, divided

1 teaspoon sugar

1 tablespoon fresh lime or lemon juice

¼ cup gin

1 cup ice, divided

1 cup Cucumber Soda (see Chapter 9)

1. Cut one spear from the section of cucumber and set aside. Coarsely chop remaining cucumber and place into a cocktail shaker.

2. Remove leaves from 1 sprig of mint and add to shaker. Add sugar and lime juice and muddle until cucumber and mint are very broken down, about 2 minutes.

3. Add gin and ½ cup ice. Shake until well blended and ice cold, about 1 minute.

4. Strain into a tall collins glass. Add remaining ½ cup ice. Top with Cucumber Soda. Garnish with remaining cucumber spear and remaining mint sprig.

Apple Cider Smash

This drink is a riff on a whiskey sour, using bourbon as the liquor but substituting lemon juice, sugar, and apple soda for the traditional sweet-sour mix. A few drops of bitters bring the flavors together.

SERVES 1

2 ounces bourbon

¼ lemon

2–3 drops bitters

¼ cup sugar, divided

1 tablespoon grenadine

½ cup ice

1 cup chilled Sour Apple Soda (see Chapter 8)

2–3 thin slices apple

1. Place bourbon, lemon, bitters, and 1 tablespoon sugar into a cocktail shaker. Muddle until lemon rind breaks down, about 1 minute. Set aside.

2. Place grenadine into a small bowl. Roll rim of a tall collins glass in grenadine. Then roll rim in reserved sugar, creating a red sugar rim.

3. Strain bourbon mixture into prepared glass. Add ice and top with soda. Garnish with apple slices.

Apples to Apples

This recipe calls for sour apple soda and apple slices as a garnish. If you're looking for a drink with a tart, singular flavor, use tart apples, like Granny Smith or Jonathan apples, as the garnish. Or, for an unexpected taste twist, use sweet apples, like Honeycrisp or Golden Delicious, as your garnish.

Sparkling Pear-Maple Cocktail

This beverage, bursting with fall flavors, is the perfect drink for any fall holiday. You'll want to use softer pears, such as Bosc, so that the cocktail has a better texture. If you happen to have any dehydrated pear slices on hand, they make a beautiful garnish. If not, the cinnamon stick will look beautiful on its own.

SERVES 1

½ soft, ripe pear (Bosc preferred)

1 tablespoon maple syrup

3 whole allspice berries

¼ cup bourbon, rye, or whiskey

½ cup ice

½ cup Pear Soda (see Chapter 8)

1 slice dehydrated pear (optional)

1 cinnamon stick

Pinch freshly grated nutmeg

1. Place pear, maple syrup, and allspice berries into the bottom of a metal cocktail shaker. Muddle together until pear is smooth, about 2 minutes.

2. Add bourbon and ice. Place top on shaker and shake to combine thoroughly, about 2 minutes.

3. Strain into a martini glass. Top with Pear Soda, and garnish with dehydrated pear slice (if using) and cinnamon stick. Sprinkle with nutmeg and serve.

Paloma

Meaning "dove" in Spanish, a Paloma is sure to keep the peace at your next warm-weather party. The traditional cocktail combines store-bought grapefruit soda with tequila. Here, you replace packaged soda with your own homemade version, and add fresh grapefruit juice, lime juice, and a hint of coriander syrup. Don't like tequila? This drink is also refreshing with vodka, rum, or gin.

SERVES 1

1 tablespoon salt, preferably a natural salt like kosher or sea salt

½ grapefruit

1 teaspoon Coriander Simple Syrup (see Chapter 10)

Juice of ¼ lime

¼ cup tequila or mescal

½ cup ice

1 cup Grapefruit Soda, either regular or low-calorie (see Chapter 6)

1. Place salt into a small saucer.

2. Cut grapefruit half into slices. Rub the rim of a tall collins glass with one slice of the grapefruit. Roll rim of the glass in salt to coat.

3. Set aside one slice grapefruit to use as a garnish. Squeeze remaining grapefruit into glass. Add Coriander Simple Syrup, lime juice, and tequila and stir.

4. Add ice and top with Grapefruit Soda. Garnish with remaining grapefruit slice.

Mescal Adds Fire to Tequila for a Smoky Note

If you like smoke and you like tequila, give mescal a try. Mescal (also spelled "mezcal") is related to tequila. Both are derived from the agave plant (a type of cactus). However, mescal differs in two major ways. Mescal uses a specific type of agave called maguey, whereas tequila uses blue agave. Also, during mescal production, the maguey is roasted, giving it a smoky taste.

Herbed Honey Punch

Punches have been around since colonial times in America, and the term "punch" is used to describe any drink that contains pieces of fruit. The first punch recipes included fruit, alcohol, sweetener, and spices. This recipe draws the fruit from your homemade lemon soda, and turns it into a punch with the addition of wine, fresh herbs, and a grating of baking spices. For a change-up, you can make this punch with Lemon Thyme Soda instead (see Chapter 9) and omit the fresh herbs.

SERVES 1

1 tablespoon honey

1 sprig fresh thyme, rosemary, sage, or mint, or a combination

¼ cup white wine or dry red wine (can be cooking wine, if desired)

½ cup Lemon Soda (see Chapter 6)

½ cup ice

Pinch ground allspice

Pinch ground nutmeg

1. Place honey and fresh herbs into the bottom of a heavy double old-fashioned glass.

2. Muddle until herbs are well broken down, about 1 minute. Pull out stems and large leaves.

3. Top mixture with wine and Lemon Soda, and stir gently.

4. Top with ice and sprinkle with allspice and nutmeg.

Sparkling Cosmopolitan

Cosmopolitans have earned their place in the list of classic cocktails. They offer a nice balance of sweet and tart, are fairly low in alcohol, and when served in a pretty martini glass, are wonderful drinks to have all evening long. This concoction is perfect for those who crave the flavors of a cosmo, but would like a bit of effervescence. This recipe switches out cranberry juice for homemade cranberry soda. Also delicious when made without the vodka.

SERVES 1

¼ cup unflavored vodka

1 tablespoon triple sec

2 teaspoons fresh lime juice

½ cup ice

½ cup or more Cranberry Soda (see Chapter 7)

1 (½" × 2") strip orange peel, orange part only

1. Place vodka, triple sec, and lime juice into a tall collins glass. Stir well.

2. Add ice and top with Cranberry Soda. Bend orange peel in half to release the essential oils. Rub the orange peel on the rim of the glass and add the orange peel to the cocktail.

Sangria

The ultimate summer punch is sangria. Bursting with fruity, citrusy flavors, lush red wine, and a hint of carbonation, this is an easy-drinking party drink. Although this recipe calls for plain homemade soda water, you could easily substitute any of the citrus sodas in this book—including the ones with herbs. If you use a fruit soda instead of club soda, omit the lemonade in this recipe.

SERVES 12

3 oranges, cut into ¾" cubes

3 lemons, cut into ¾" cubes

3 limes, cut into ¾" cubes

½ cup brandy

¼ cup triple sec

2 cups orange juice

2 cups lemonade (preferably not made from a powdered mix)

2 (750-milliliter) bottles dry red wine, such as Burgundy,
Cabernet Sauvignon, Rioja, or Zinfandel

1 quart chilled homemade club soda

1. In a medium, nonreactive bowl or pot, combine orange, lemon, lime, brandy, and triple sec. Cover and let sit at room temperature for 1 hour to allow flavors to meld.

2. Strain fruit from liquid. Set fruit aside to use as a garnish. Place strained liquid into a large pitcher. Add orange juice, lemonade, wine, and club soda.

3. To serve, fill a wine glass with ice. Add ¼ cup of reserved fruit and top with wine mixture.

Substituting Herbal Sodas into Sangria

When substituting an herbal soda for the club soda in this recipe, the trick is to make sure the herb works well with the other citrus fruit. Lemon Thyme Soda, Lime Basil Soda, and Grapefruit Sage Sodas are all excellent substitutions. Steer clear of Orange Lavender Soda here. The floral taste competes with the other flavors in this punch.

CHAPTER 12

Foods Made with Carbonated Beverages

Never heard of adding carbonated beverages to foods? Wait till you see what you've been missing! Carbonated beverages add fluffiness to baked goods like quick breads and cakes, and they make breakfast foods like pancakes, waffles, and omelets a snap to prepare. You'll even love the tanginess that your own homemade sodas add to favorite savory foods like baked beans and fried chicken.

Fluffy Pancakes

The addition of carbonated water to a pancake batter creates fluffy, tender pancakes. The secret is to mix all the dry ingredients together, then mix the wet ingredients together separately, and barely blend the two before cooking the pancakes. This will ensure that the gluten (the wheat protein) in the flour will stay relaxed, keeping the pancakes soft and fluffy.

SERVES 4–6

1¾ cups all-purpose flour

1 tablespoon baking powder

½ teaspoon salt, preferably a natural salt like kosher or sea salt

1 egg

½ cup unsalted butter, melted

2 cups homemade club soda

Pan spray

1. In a medium bowl, mix together flour, baking powder, and salt until thoroughly blended. In a separate medium mixing bowl, mix egg, butter, and club soda until well blended.

2. Slowly add wet ingredients to dry ingredients, taking breaks if the mixture bubbles too much. Once you have added all wet ingredients, stir with a wooden spoon until barely mixed, about 5–10 stirs. You may still see lumps of flour within the pancake batter.

3. Heat a large skillet over medium heat until hot. Spray with pan spray and add ¼-cup scoops of pancake batter until you have 3–4 pancakes in the skillet. When pancakes have holes in the side facing up, flip each pancake, about 3–4 minutes. Cook until pancakes are golden brown on each side, an additional 3 minutes.

4. Repeat with remaining pancake batter. Serve pancakes with butter, syrup, and jelly.

Dairy-Free Waffles

According to legend, this recipe was originally created by a parent of a child with a dairy allergy. Instead of using butter and milk (as is called for in traditional waffle recipes), it uses home-carbonated soda and vegetable oil. If you prefer, you can always substitute butter for the oil in this recipe.

SERVES 3–4

1¾ cups all-purpose flour

1 tablespoon baking powder

1 teaspoon salt, preferably a natural salt like kosher or sea salt

2 tablespoons sugar

2 eggs

⅓ cup neutral vegetable oil, such as canola, safflower, or sunflower seed oil

1½ cups homemade club soda

Pan spray (optional)

1. Preheat your waffle iron using manufacturer's directions.

2. In a medium bowl, combine dry ingredients until well blended. In a separate bowl, beat egg with canola oil. Slowly add club soda and stir just to combine.

3. Slowly add wet ingredients to dry ingredients, taking breaks if the mixture bubbles too much. Once you have added all wet ingredients, stir with a wooden spoon until barely mixed, about 5–10 stirs. You may still see lumps of flour within the waffle batter.

4. Spray the surface of waffle iron with pan spray, if manufacturer's instructions recommend doing so. Pour ¾ cup of waffle batter onto waffle maker. Cook waffle according to manufacturer's instructions. Serve with margarine, butter, jelly, and/or syrup.

Make Your Own Toaster-Ready Waffles

While it's great to have waffles straight off the waffle iron, you don't always have time to make them. One solution is to undercook a few waffles and freeze them. When you've made all the waffles you want for breakfast on a given day, reduce the heat setting on your waffle iron by one or two marks. Cook waffles until they are very light brown, yet still solid. Cool to room temperature; then double-wrap in plastic and freeze. To serve frozen waffles, toast them in your toaster or toaster oven as you would store-bought frozen waffles.

Best-Ever Basic Omelet

Why is it that when you have an omelet in a restaurant, it's impossibly light and fluffy, while your homemade omelet is thin and flat in comparison? Now you'll be able to replicate the results you have at your favorite breakfast place in your own kitchen. The addition of homemade club soda and a pinch of baking powder helps your omelets to rise. But beware—if word of your tall, fluffy omelets reaches the neighbors, you may have lines forming at your kitchen door on the weekend.

SERVES 2

5 large eggs

2 tablespoons homemade club soda

Pinch baking powder

½ teaspoon salt, preferably a natural salt like kosher or sea salt

¼ teaspoon freshly ground black pepper

1 tablespoon butter, or 2–3 sprays pan spray

1 cup of your favorite filling, such as chopped ham, cooked vegetables, shredded cheese, crumbled bacon, and/or fresh herbs

1. Place eggs, club soda, baking powder, salt, and pepper into the bowl of a blender or food processor. Blend on high for 20–30 seconds.

2. Heat a large skillet over medium-high heat. Place filling into pan and cook, stirring often, until heated through, about 30–45 seconds. Transfer filling to a clean plate, keeping it close to the stove. (Note: If you use cheese or fresh herbs in your filling, don't heat them at this time. Instead, you'll simply add them at the end, when the heat of the cooked omelet will melt the cheese and/or warm the herbs.)

3. Wipe the pan clean with a paper towel and return pan to the stove. Turn on medium-high heat and melt butter in pan or spray pan with pan spray. Begin shaking pan back and forth on the burner. Add egg and scramble until the egg is halfway cooked, about 1 minute.

4. Turn heat to medium-low and add filling to one half of the omelet. Allow the omelet to cook until lightly brown on one side, and turn the unfilled half over the filled half. Cook until the egg is no longer runny, about 1 more minute.

Fabulous Fondue

This is an alcohol-free version of traditional fondue. Typically, fondue calls for white wine and kirsch, a clear cherry spirit. Here, you substitute cherry soda for the wine and kirsch. To keep the fondue from sticking and burning on the bottom of your pot, stir the cheese with your skewer as you eat.

SERVES 8

1 clove garlic, peeled and cut in half

1½ cups or 1 (12-ounce) can evaporated milk

1 cup Cherry Soda (see Chapter 7)

2–3 dashes hot pepper sauce, or to taste

2–3 dashes Worcestershire sauce, or to taste

¼ cup all-purpose flour

½ teaspoon dry mustard

4 ounces Swiss cheese, shredded

4 ounces Fontina cheese, shredded

Freshly ground black pepper (optional)

1. Rub the inside of fondue pot with garlic halves and discard. (For a stronger garlic flavor, leave garlic in the pot and use a slotted spoon to remove them just before adding the cheese.) Add milk, Cherry Soda, hot pepper sauce, and Worcestershire sauce to pot. Heat pot over high to bring to a boil.

2. Meanwhile, add flour, dry mustard, and both cheeses to a large resealable bag. Seal and shake to mix well. Pour the contents of the bag into fondue pot and stir to combine. Cook on low until heated through and cheese has melted, stirring occasionally.

3. Taste for seasoning, adding hot sauce, Worcestershire sauce, and/or pepper, if desired.

Fabulous Fondue Serving Suggestions

Cheese fondue is traditionally served with bread cubes that are each pierced with a fondue fork and dipped into the fondue. Steamed or roasted asparagus spears and raw or cooked baby carrots, broccoli florets, cauliflower florets, pickle slices, radishes, snow peas, and sweet bell pepper strips are also delicious dipped in a savory fondue sauce.

Tempura with Shrimp, Sweet Potatoes, and Green Beans

Deep-fried vegetables and shrimp, known as tempura, are traditional Japanese fare. The batter is extremely crisp, due in large part to the sparkling water used in the recipe. Also essential is keeping the batter chilled while working with it, and stirring the batter just enough. In this recipe, you'll keep the batter in a bowl over another bowl of ice water, and stir the batter minimally.

SERVES 4

½ cup water

½ cup soy sauce

½ cup mirin (rice wine)

2 scallions, stemmed and finely diced

4–6 cups canola oil

2 cups well-chilled homemade club soda

¼ cup vodka

1 teaspoon salt, preferably a natural salt like kosher or sea salt

2 cups all-purpose flour

½ pound fresh green beans, washed, trimmed, and cut into 2" pieces

1 medium sweet potato, peeled, cut in half lengthwise, and cut into ¼" slices

½ pound raw shrimp, peeled, deveined, tails removed

1. Make the tempura dipping sauce: Mix together water, soy sauce, mirin, and scallions. Set aside.

2. Line a rimmed baking sheet with a double layer of paper towels.

3. Place 4 cups oil into a deep, heavy pot. (The depth of the oil should be at least 3". If necessary, add more oil to reach this depth.) Heat until hot, but not smoking, over high heat, about 10 minutes. If you have a candy thermometer, the temperature of the oil should reach 375°F.

4. Mix club soda and vodka together in a glass measuring cup with spout.

5. Fill a large bowl halfway with ice water. In a separate medium bowl, combine salt and flour. Nest the bowl containing flour mixture into the ice water bowl.

6. Add club soda mixture and stir until just combined, about 5–10 stirs.

7. Working in batches, dip green beans into batter, allowing excess to drip off. Immediately fry in oil until golden and crisp, about 3–4 minutes. Transfer cooked green beans to lined baking sheet.

8. Repeat with sweet potatoes, and then shrimp. Serve tempura with dipping sauce.

Spiced Lentils with Ethiopian Flatbread

The cuisine of Ethiopia is a delicate balance of African and Indian influences. Rich sauces with legumes, vegetables, and meats cover sponge-like pancakes called injera bread, which gets its texture from the addition of homemade club soda. Part of the joy of eating Ethiopian food is eating without utensils, instead using extra pieces of injera bread to pick up food.

SERVES 6–8

1 cup lentils

2 tablespoons neutral vegetable oil, like canola, safflower, or sunflower seed oil

½ medium red onion, diced

5 cloves garlic, minced, or 1 tablespoon garlic paste

1 (1") piece fresh ginger, peeled and grated, or 1 tablespoon ginger paste

1 tablespoon paprika

1 teaspoon red pepper flakes

½ teaspoon cumin powder

½ teaspoon cardamom powder

½ teaspoon turmeric

½ teaspoon cinnamon

Pinch ground cloves

Pinch ground allspice

3 cups cold water

1 teaspoon salt, preferably a natural salt like kosher or sea salt

½ teaspoon black pepper

2 cups warm water

2 cups self-rising flour

¼ cup homemade club soda

1. Place lentils into a wire-mesh sieve. Pick through lentils, removing any small stones, debris, or chunks of dirt you find. Rinse lentils well and set aside.

2. Heat a medium heavy saucepot or Dutch oven over medium heat. Add oil, onion, garlic, and ginger. Cook, stirring frequently, until onions are translucent and tender, about 5–7 minutes.

3. Sprinkle with paprika, red pepper flakes, cumin, cardamom, turmeric, cinnamon, cloves, and allspice, and cook, stirring constantly, until spices release their flavor, an additional 1–2 minutes.

4. Add lentils and cold water. Cover and bring to a boil. Remove cover, reduce heat to low, and simmer until lentils are cooked through, about 30–40 minutes. Season with salt and pepper and keep warm until ready to serve.

5. Make injera bread: Heat a large, nonstick skillet over medium heat until hot.

6. Put warm water and flour into the bowl of a blender or food processor. Pulse 5–10 times to roughly combine; then blend at full speed for 30 seconds to mix well.

7. Transfer mixture to a bowl with a pour spout (or a large glass measuring cup). Slowly add club soda, taking care to stop if the mixture starts bubbling too much. Stir gently to combine.

8. Pour ¼ cup of batter onto hot pan and swirl to coat entire bottom of pan with batter. Cook until bread looks like a sponge and is dry to the touch. Remove, placing cooked bread into a basket lined with a clean kitchen towel. Repeat with remaining batter.

9. To serve, line a platter with a single layer of injera bread. Mound lentils atop bread and serve, passing additional bread to guests to use for scooping up the lentil mixture and eating.

Homemade Self-Rising Flour

Self-rising flour is the same as all-purpose flour, with the addition of rising agents. If you don't have store-bought self-rising flour, you can make the amount you need for this recipe by sifting together 2 cups all-purpose flour, 1 tablespoon baking powder, and ½ teaspoon salt.

Club Soda Banana Bread

Banana bread is one of the best ways to use up bananas that are too ripe and mushy to eat as fruit in hand. One common complaint about banana bread, however, is that it's dense and too chewy. With the addition of club soda to your recipe, you lighten the banana bread. This recipe is so tasty, you'll be tempted to let all your bananas ripen a few days too long, just so you can make more banana bread.

SERVES 12

2 ripe bananas

2 eggs

1 cup sugar

½ cup canola oil

1 teaspoon vanilla extract

2 tablespoons nonfat Greek yogurt

¼ cup homemade club soda

2 cups all-purpose flour

1 teaspoon baking powder

1¼ teaspoons baking soda

½ teaspoon salt, preferably a natural salt like kosher or sea salt

½ cup toasted walnut or pecan pieces (optional)

1. Preheat oven to 350°F. Spray two loaf pans with pan spray.

2. Peel bananas and place into a large bowl. Mash with a potato masher or fork. Add eggs, sugar, oil, vanilla, and yogurt. Beat until smooth, about 2 minutes. Slowly add club soda and stir to combine.

3. Fold a 12" × 12" sheet of parchment paper or waxed paper in half and open (paper should have a deep crease). Sift together flour, baking powder, baking soda, and salt onto the open paper.

4. With the mixer running on low speed, add dry ingredients into wet ingredients. Mix until just blended. Stir in nuts, if using.

5. Pour half of batter into each pan. Bake until a toothpick inserted into the center of each loaf comes out clean, about 30 to 35 minutes.

6. Let cool completely. Unmold from pans, slice, and serve.

Cola-Brined Fried Chicken

Making your own fried chicken at home can be difficult. The challenge is to get a crisp crust and cook the chicken all the way through, without drying out the meat. Brining the chicken prior to breading and frying it helps to keep the meat moist. Your homemade cola adds the right amount of sweetness and complexity to the brine. The addition of soda water to the batter lightens it up and gives the crust an airy crispness.

SERVES 4–6

1 whole frying chicken (about 4 pounds), cut into wings, thighs, legs, and breasts

4–6 cups Cola (see Chapter 5; use
cola with sugar, not a noncaloric sweetener)

⅓ cup salt, preferably a natural salt like kosher or sea salt

10 cloves garlic, peeled and crushed

1 egg

1 teaspoon baking powder

½ teaspoon baking soda

½ cup homemade club soda

½ cup buttermilk

4–6 cups all-purpose flour

4 cups canola or peanut oil

1. Rinse chicken pieces under hot water and pat dry with paper towel. Using a large, sharp knife, cut the wing tips off each wing and discard, or reserve for another use. Cut each breast crosswise into two even pieces. (Each piece should be roughly the same size as the chicken thigh.)

2. In a large, nonreactive bowl, mix 4 cups Cola, salt, and garlic. Stir until salt dissolves, about 2 minutes. Add chicken pieces to brine. Add more Cola if chicken pieces are not completely submerged. Cover bowl tightly with plastic wrap and place in the lowest part of your refrigerator. Let chicken marinate for 3 hours.

3. Place a baking rack on a rimmed baking sheet. Using tongs, remove each piece of chicken from the brine and place onto rack. Pat excess brine from chicken using paper towels. Leave chicken uncovered and return chicken with rack and baking sheet to the refrigerator. Chill, uncovered, for 3 hours.

4. Place egg, baking powder, and baking soda into a medium mixing bowl. Whisk briefly to combine. Slowly whisk in club soda and buttermilk, stopping occasionally to let the mixture bubble. Once you've added all club soda and buttermilk, slowly whisk mixture to combine. Set aside.

5. Place 4 cups flour into a separate, large bowl. Dip each piece of chicken into flour, coating completely and shaking off excess. Return chicken to rack.

6. Dip each piece of chicken into egg mixture, coating completely and allowing excess egg to drip off. Return chicken to rack.

7. Dip each piece of chicken into flour a second time, coating completely and shaking off excess. Return chicken to rack.

8. Preheat oven to 375°F.

9. Place oil into a cast-iron skillet or an iron or enameled iron Dutch oven. Heat over high heat until oil begins to smoke, about 10 minutes.

10. Working in batches, place 3–4 pieces of chicken into hot oil. Chicken should be in a single layer, and not touching. (Note: Hot oil should sputter and bubble when you add chicken. If it doesn't, the oil is not hot enough. Remove chicken from the oil and continue to heat the oil until it's hot enough.)

11. Cook the chicken until each piece is deep golden brown on one side, about 4 minutes. Using metal tongs, turn chicken and cook until other side is deep golden brown, about 3 minutes. Transfer each piece of fried chicken to rack on baking sheet. Repeat frying process with remaining chicken.

12. Place baking sheet into oven and bake until chicken reaches 165°F on a meat thermometer, about 15–20 minutes. Serve immediately.

Grilled Steak Kebabs

If you want to kick up the "grilled" flavor of your dishes, add some tea, which has a natural, smoky flavor. Here, barbecue sauce gets a boost from sparkling iced tea. Especially delicious when you use the Cherry Cola Barbecue Sauce from this chapter.

SERVES 4

1 pound tender steak, such as tenderloin or filet mignon

¾ cup barbecue sauce

½ cup Sparkling Iced Tea, unsweetened (see Chapter 10)

¼ teaspoon ground black pepper

8 ounces cremini mushrooms

2 red bell peppers, cut into 1-inch cubes

1. Combine steak cubes with barbecue sauce, Sparkling Iced Tea, and pepper in a medium bowl. Massage the marinade into the meat with your hands; let stand for 10 minutes.

2. Meanwhile, prepare vegetables and preheat grill. Thread steak cubes, mushrooms, and bell peppers onto metal skewers and place on grill over medium coals.

3. Grill, covered, brushing frequently with remaining marinade, for 7–10 minutes, turning frequently, until steak reaches desired doneness. Discard any remaining marinade. Serve immediately.

Grill Temperatures

Check the temperature of your grill by carefully holding your hand about 6 inches above the coals and counting how many seconds you can hold your hand steady before it gets too hot. If you can hold your hand for 5 seconds, the coals are low; 4 seconds, medium; 3 seconds, medium-high; and 2 seconds, high.

Cola-Cravin' Ground Beef

If you prefer tomato sauce that's extra meaty and slightly sweet, this sauce is for you. Your own homemade cola adds the right sweetness, plus hints of citrus and fennel, to make a delicious sauce. Great over pasta, or in a lasagna. Or, for a quick weeknight supper, use as a topping for baked potatoes. And if you don't eat beef, ground turkey is a tasty substitute.

SERVES 8

3 pounds lean ground beef or lean ground turkey

2 teaspoons salt, divided

2 tablespoons extra-virgin olive oil

1 large sweet onion, peeled and diced

2 cloves garlic, peeled and minced

1 cup Cola (see Chapter 5)

1 (28-ounce) can tomato purée

1 large handful fresh basil leaves, slivered

1. Place ground beef into a large nonstick skillet and sprinkle with 1 teaspoon salt. Cook over medium heat, breaking apart the meat as you do so. Remove and discard any fat rendered from the meat. Transfer meat to a slow cooker.

2. Add oil and onion to same large skillet (don't clean pan first—you'll want the flavor of the beef to flavor the onions) and sprinkle with remaining salt. Cook over medium heat until onion is transparent, about 8 minutes. Stir in garlic and cook until fragrant, about 30 seconds to 1 minute. Transfer to slow cooker.

3. Add Cola and tomato purée. Stir to combine. Cover and cook on low until flavors melt, about 4 to 6 hours. Stir in basil and cook an additional 20 minutes. Serve.

Lemongrass Soda–Brined Pork Chops with Mint-Basil-Cilantro Pesto

When you're craving the exotic taste of Southeast Asia, you can't go wrong with this dish. Blending the bold flavor of lemongrass with succulent pork, and a three-herb pesto, you'll find this will be your go-to dish when you're looking to impress guests. Round out the meal by serving cooked rice noodles and a green papaya salad.

SERVES 4

4–6 cups Lemongrass Soda (see Chapter 9)

⅓ cup salt, preferably a natural salt like kosher or sea salt

4 bone-in pork chops, 1½–2" thick

¼ cup fresh mint leaves

¼ cup fresh basil leaves

¼ cup fresh cilantro leaves

1 clove garlic

4 tablespoons canola oil, divided

1 teaspoon fish sauce

1 tablespoon white sugar

1. In a large, resealable bag, mix 4 cups Lemongrass Soda with salt. Stir until salt dissolves, about 2 minutes. Add pork chops to brine. Add more soda if chops are not completely submerged. Zip closed and place in the lowest part of your refrigerator. Let pork marinate for 2–3 hours.

2. Place a baking rack on a rimmed baking sheet. Using tongs, remove each pork chop from brine and place onto rack. Pat excess brine from chops using paper towels. Leave chops uncovered and return chops with rack and baking sheet to the refrigerator. Chill, uncovered, for 3 hours.

3. Meanwhile, make pesto. Place mint, basil, cilantro, garlic, 3 tablespoons oil, fish sauce, and sugar into the bowl of a food processor or blender. Purée until smooth, about 1 minute. Transfer to a bowl and set aside.

4. Preheat oven to 350°F. Remove pork chops from refrigerator.

5. Heat a large ovensafe skillet over medium-high heat. Add remaining canola oil and heat until hot, but not smoking. Add pork chops in a single, even layer. Cook until deep brown on one side, about 7–8 minutes.

6. Turn pork and cook until deep brown on second side, about 3–4 minutes.

7. Transfer pan to oven and bake uncovered until pork reaches 145°F on a meat thermometer, about 5–7 minutes.

8. Remove pork from oven and allow to rest 5 minutes. Serve with pesto.

Matzo Ball Soup

Light and fluffy matzo balls are easier to achieve when you put your at-home carbonator to work. The bubbles in the soda expand within the matzo balls, improving their texture. The soup calls for turmeric, a dried root that's similar to ginger. It adds a bit of flavor to the soup, and really brings out the rich yellow color of a good chicken broth.

SERVES 8

1 (4–5 pound) whole chicken, cut into 3" × 3" pieces

4 celery stalks, sliced into ½" slices

4 carrots, chopped

2 yellow or white onions, chopped

1½ tablespoons salt, preferably a natural salt like kosher or sea salt, divided

3 sprigs fresh parsley

3 sprigs fresh thyme

1 teaspoon black peppercorns

1 bay leaf

1 teaspoon turmeric

¼ cup homemade club soda

½ teaspoon black pepper

4 large eggs

½ teaspoon baking soda

1 cup matzo meal

1. Preheat the oven to 450°F. Spread the chicken, celery, carrots, and onions in a single, even layer across two or more rimmed baking sheets. Bake chicken and vegetables, checking and stirring the ingredients every 15 minutes, until everything is a rich, deep color, about 40 minutes.

2. Measure 2 tablespoons of the rendered chicken fat from the pan and set aside. Transfer chicken, vegetables, 1 tablespoon salt, parsley, thyme, peppercorns, bay leaf, and turmeric to a deep stock pot. Add water to cover ingredients by 1". Bring to a boil; then reduce heat to low and simmer, uncovered, for 5–6 hours.

3. Strain broth through a wire-mesh sieve, pressing on solids with the back of a spoon to release liquid. When cool enough to handle, remove chicken from bones and chop into bite-size pieces. Transfer to a container, cover, and refrigerate until you're ready to serve soup.

4. Discard bones, skin, and remaining solids.

5. Cool liquid to room temperature, about an hour. Cover, transfer to refrigerator, and chill overnight (along with reserved chicken fat).

6. Remove floating fat from top of chicken broth and discard.

7. Whisk together reserved chicken fat, club soda, remaining salt, pepper, and eggs in a medium mixing bowl. In a separate bowl, mix baking soda and matzo meal. Add dry ingredients to wet ingredients and stir 10–15 times to just barely combine. Cover and transfer to refrigerator. Chill for 1 hour or more.

8. When you would like to serve the soup, transfer broth to a large stock pot and bring to a boil. Reduce heat and simmer broth uncovered as you form the matzo balls.

9. Remove matzo mixture from refrigerator. Fill a medium bowl with cold water. Dip your hands into the water so that your hands are wet. Take about 2 tablespoons matzo mixture and roll into a ball. Repeat with remaining matzo mixture. Gently transfer matzo balls to simmering broth.

10. Simmer, uncovered, until cooked through, about 45–60 minutes. Add reserved chicken and heat until warmed through, about 5 minutes. Serve soup.

Use Your Slow Cooker!

Instead of cooking the chicken as described in the first two steps, you may also cook the chicken broth in a slow cooker. Place ingredients into slow cooker and cook on low for 8–10 hours.

Root Beer Baked Beans

Making baked beans from scratch is worth the extra effort, especially since your oven or your slow cooker will do most of the work. And this baked beans recipe is quick to assemble when you have homemade root beer on hand—the soft drink adds just the right sweetness and spice to the beans. If you find that this recipe makes more beans than you need at one time, don't worry. Baked beans freeze and reheat nicely.

SERVES 8

1 pound dried butter, kidney, navy, or pinto beans (or any combination of beans)

3 tablespoons canola oil

1 medium yellow or white onion, diced

1 clove garlic, minced

2 cups Root Beer (see Chapter 5)

3 cups water

1 teaspoon dry mustard

2 tablespoons tomato paste

2 tablespoons cider vinegar

2 teaspoons salt, preferably a natural salt like kosher or sea salt

½ teaspoon ground black pepper

Pinch dried hot pepper powder

1. Place beans in a wire-mesh strainer and rinse under cold running water. Transfer to a large pot and cover with cold water by 2". Bring to a boil and turn off heat. Soak for 1 hour.

2. Preheat oven to 350°F. Heat a large Dutch oven over medium heat. Add oil and onions and cook, stirring frequently, until onions soften, about 8 minutes. Add garlic and cook until garlic is fragrant, about 30 seconds–1 minute.

3. Drain beans and add to Dutch oven, along with Root Beer, water, mustard, and tomato paste. Stir well to combine. Cover pot, transfer to oven, and bake until beans are tender, about 6–8 hours.

4. Transfer beans to stovetop and place over medium heat. Remove lid and simmer until most of the liquid is absorbed, about 10 minutes. Stir in vinegar, salt, pepper, and hot pepper powder. Simmer an additional 10 minutes, adjusting seasoning if necessary.

Use Your Slow Cooker!

You can also make beans in a slow cooker. Rinse and soak the beans, and cook the vegetables as directed in this recipe. Then instead of cooking in your oven, place beans in a slow cooker with the rest of the ingredients, and cook on high, covered, for 4–6 hours until beans are very tender. Once the beans are tender, remove the cover from your slow cooker and cook until excess water has evaporated, about 20 minutes. (This takes longer than over the stove because the slow cooker is at a lower heat.)

Cherry Cola Barbecue Sauce

Armed with homemade cherry cola, you have a secret ingredient to add to any sweet-tangy dish. The combination of fruit and spice is intriguing and will have your diners asking what you put into your recipe. You'll find that it's especially delicious in this barbecue sauce, which is good on chicken, beef, or pork. If you like a hint of spice, add the optional chipotle pepper.

SERVES 8

2 tablespoons canola oil

1 large yellow or white onion, chopped

2 cloves garlic, minced

3 cups ketchup

½ pound cherries, pitted

2 cups Cherry Cola (regular, not diet; see Chapter 5)

1 chipotle pepper in adobo sauce (optional)

¼ cup cider vinegar

½ teaspoon salt, preferably a natural salt like kosher or sea salt

¼ teaspoon ground black pepper

1. Place oil into a large saucepan over medium heat. Add onions and cook until softened, about 8 minutes. Add garlic and cook until fragrant, about 30 seconds–1 minute.

2. Add ketchup, cherries, Cherry Cola, chipotle (if using), and vinegar and bring to a boil. Reduce heat and simmer, uncovered, stirring occasionally, until cherries are completely softened, about 1 hour.

3. Transfer to the bowl of a food processor or blender. Place top onto food processor or blender and pulse 10–15 times, ensuring that the lid stays on (the heat from the mixture will release steam, which will lift off the lid). Then blend on high until completely smooth, about 2 minutes.

4. Season to taste with salt and pepper. Transfer to storage container and cool completely.

Lemon-Lime Pound Cake

Buttery pound cake has a natural affinity for citrus. The addition of homemade lemon-lime soda and two citrus zests really turns up the flavor in this dessert. Use this recipe as a basis to experiment with different citrus blends. Simply substitute a different type of soda for the lemon-lime soda, and swap out the citrus zests. Try it with grapefruit soda!

SERVES 8

Pan spray
½ pound (2 sticks) unsalted butter
1 cup sugar
3 eggs
3 egg yolks (whites can be reserved for another use)
2 tablespoons Lemon-Lime Soda (see Chapter 5)
½ teaspoon salt, preferably a natural salt like kosher or sea salt
1½ cups all-purpose flour
Zest of ½ lemon, finely grated
Zest of ½ lime, finely grated

1. Preheat oven to 325°F. Spray a loaf pan with pan spray.

2. Place butter and sugar together into a large mixing bowl. Cream together with a mixer until sugar is completely dissolved and mixture is fluffy, about 5 minutes.

3. With mixer running, add eggs and egg yolks one at a time. Do not add an egg or yolk until the previous one is fully incorporated into mixture. Slowly add Lemon-Lime Soda.

4. Fold a 12" × 12" sheet of parchment paper or waxed paper in half and open (paper should have a deep crease). Sift together salt and flour onto the open paper. Top with both citrus zests.

5. With mixer on low speed, slowly add dry ingredients to bowl, using the crease in the paper as a funnel. When all ingredients are added, turn off mixer.

6. Transfer batter to prepared pan and bake until toothpick comes out clean when inserted into middle, about 1 hour–1 hour and 15 minutes.

7. Remove cake from oven and cool 5 minutes in pan on a wire rack. Remove cake from pan and cool to room temperature on wire rack for 1 hour.

8. Cut into slices and serve.

Chocolate Chip Red Velvet Cupcakes

Everyone loves to guard a secret ingredient. This one is surely a treasure: No one will guess that soda pop is the magic-maker in this moist cupcake. Sprinkle just a dusting of cocoa powder on these cupcakes for a decadent extra touch.

MAKES 24 CUPCAKES

2 egg whites
1 (18.25-ounce) box red velvet cake mix
1 cup white chocolate chips
¾ cup Lemon-Lime Soda (see Chapter 5)
Your favorite sour cream frosting

1. Preheat oven to 350°F. Line a muffin tin with paper baking cups.

2. Combine egg whites, cake mix, chocolate chips, and soda in a large mixing bowl. Mix well until a smooth batter forms. Pour batter into baking cups, filling each cup halfway.

3. Bake for 20–25 minutes, until a toothpick inserted into the center of a cupcake comes out clean. Cool completely. Remove from muffin tin. Frost and serve.

Pistachio Cupcakes

These green treats are too cute for words! They're easy to whip up for a St. Patrick's Day or Christmas party. Your own homemade Lemon-Lime Soda makes them extra fluffy.

MAKES 24 CUPCAKES

1 (14- to 18-ounce) package white cake mix (different brands have different sizes—they will all pretty much work the same)

2 eggs or 3 egg whites

¼ cup vegetable oil

1 cup Lemon-Lime Soda (see Chapter 5)

1 (3- to 4-ounce) package pistachio instant pudding mix (different brands have different sizes—they will all pretty much work the same)

Your favorite white buttercream frosting

1. Preheat oven to 350°F. Line a muffin tin with paper baking cups. Set aside.

2. Place all ingredients, except frosting, in a large bowl. Beat together for 3 minutes with an electric beater set on medium speed. Fill muffin cups half-full. Bake for 20–25 minutes, until a toothpick inserted into the center of a cupcake comes out clean.

3. Cool completely. Remove from muffin tin. Frost and serve.

Spiced Bundt Cake

Simple fizz cake gets a little fancy in this still-simple recipe. Four ingredients are all it takes to bake up a beautiful cake.

SERVES 12

Pan spray
1 (16- to 18-ounce) box chocolate cake mix
1½ cups Root Beer (see Chapter 5)
1 cup raisins or walnuts
Bundt Cake Glaze (recipe follows)

1. Preheat oven according to package instructions. Spray Bundt pan with pan spray.

2. Gently stir together cake mix and soda. Do not overstir; you want to preserve the soda's fizz. Stir in raisins or nuts. Pour mixture into prepared pan. Bake according to cake mix instructions.

3. Cool cake 10 minutes, then remove from pan and allow to cool completely, about 1 hour. Pour Bundt Cake Glaze over cake.

Bundt Cake Glaze

½ cup dark chocolate chips
¼ cup unsalted butter
1 tablespoon light corn syrup

Mix ingredients together in a small microwave-safe bowl or a 1-cup microwave-safe glass measuring cup. Cook on medium power until melted, stopping every 30 seconds to stir mixture, about 2 minutes. Drizzle over cake while sauce is still warm and liquid.

Fruity Angel Food Cookies

These bright and yummy cookies are tempting treats that are relatively low in calories. Use any fruit-flavored soda—even the reduced-calorie varieties. Citrus soda adds a lovely tartness to these cookies, while other fruit flavors add sweetness. Or try this recipe with Orange Cream Soda (see Chapter 5) or Orange Ginger Ale (see Chapter 6) for a decadent twist. Regardless of the type you choose, you'll find the addition of soda makes these cookies light as air.

MAKES 25–30 COOKIES

Pan spray
1 (14- to 16-ounce) box angel food cake mix
½ cup your favorite regular or low-calorie fruit soda
¼ teaspoon almond extract

1. Preheat oven to 350°F. Spray rimmed baking sheets with pan spray.

2. Combine cake mix, soda, and almond extract in a large mixing bowl using an electric mixer set to medium speed. Mix to form a smooth, fully incorporated dough.

3. Using a tablespoon, drop dough onto baking sheets, leaving 1 inch around each cookie. You should have 25–30 cookies in total. Bake until cookies are light golden, about 8–10 minutes. Remove from baking sheet to a wire rack for cooling. Serve and enjoy.

Strawberry Soda Pop Cake

This cake is based on a homespun recipe with origins in the southern United States. Like many recipes developed by home cooks, there are a number of variations. Some call for strawberry cake mix, some for strawberry Jell-O. However, all have strawberry soda pop as one of the ingredients. In this recipe, you'll make a cake from scratch, using your own strawberry soda, plus some of the undiluted base as a liquid. Then you'll top the cake with whipped cream and fresh strawberries.

SERVES 8

Pan spray

2 cups cake flour, divided

1 cup sugar

2 teaspoons baking powder

½ teaspoon salt, preferably a natural salt like kosher or sea salt

3 eggs

1 teaspoon vanilla extract

1½ sticks butter, melted then cooled to room temperature

1 cup Strawberry Soda (see Chapter 7)

¼ cup Strawberry Soda base, undiluted (see Chapter 7)

2 cups chilled whipping cream

½ cup sugar

1 pound fresh strawberries, washed, hulled, and sliced

1. Spray two 9" cake pans with pan spray. Take ¼ cup of cake flour and swirl it inside each pan, coating well. Discard excess flour used to coat pans.

2. Preheat oven to 350°F. Fold a 12" × 12" sheet of parchment paper or waxed paper in half and open (paper should have a deep crease). Sift together remaining flour, sugar, baking powder, and salt onto the open paper. Set aside.

3. Place eggs, vanilla extract, and butter into a medium bowl or the bowl of a stand mixer. Beat on high until eggs are well scrambled, about 1 minute. Turn mixer to low speed and slowly add Strawberry Soda.

4. With mixer on low speed, slowly add dry ingredients to bowl, using the crease in the paper as a funnel. When all ingredients are added, turn off mixer. If ingredients aren't fully mixed, gently fold together with a spoon.

5. Divide batter between prepared cake pans and bake until a toothpick inserted into the center of each cake comes out clean, about 20–25 minutes.

6. Remove cakes from oven and cool on a wire rack for 5 minutes. Turn each cake out of its pan and cool completely to room temperature, about 1 hour.

7. Meanwhile, make frosting: Whip cream on high until foamy. With mixer running, slowly add sugar. Continue beating until stiff peaks form, about 7 minutes.

8. Place one cooled cake onto a cake plate. Top with ¾ cup whipped cream. Smooth over top of cake. Top with 1 cup strawberry slices. Place second cake on top of frosted cake. Top with ¾ cup whipped cream. Smooth. Frost sides of cake with remaining frosting and decorate cake with remaining strawberries. Serve.

Cake Flour

This recipe calls for cake flour, which is slightly different from all-purpose flour, the flour you find most often. Cake flour contains less gluten (the protein found in wheat). You can make your own cake flour, though. For each cup of flour, remove 2 tablespoons of flour and replace with 2 tablespoons cornstarch. Mix the flour and cornstarch well, then sift. Voilà! Cake flour!

APPENDIX

Resources

Soda-Making Machines and Equipment

Amazon.com
www.amazon.com

Bed Bath & Beyond
www.bedbathandbeyond.com

Bloomingdale's
www.bloomingdales.com

Cuisinart
www.cuisinart.com

Home Shopping Network
www.hsn.com

iSi
www.isi.com/culinary/us

Kohl's
www.kohls.com

Lowe's
www.lowes.com

Macy's
www.macys.com

QVC
www.qvc.com

SodaStream
www.sodastream.com

Sur La Table
www.surlatable.com

Target
www.target.com

Walmart
www.walmart.com

Williams-Sonoma
www.williams-sonoma.com

Ingredients

Amazon.com
www.amazon.com

Amigo Foods
www.amigofoods.com

Asian Food Grocer
www.asianfoodgrocer.com

Bulk Apothecary
www.bulkapothecary.com

Goya
www.goya.com

H Mart
www.hmart.com

Latin Merchant
www.latinmerchant.com

Penzeys Spices
www.penzeys.com

Vitamin Shoppe
www.vitaminshoppe.com

Wegmans
www.wegmans.com

Whole Foods Market
www.wholefoodsmarket.com

STANDARD U.S./METRIC MEASUREMENT CONVERSIONS

VOLUME CONVERSIONS	
U.S. Volume Measure	Metric Equivalent
⊠ teaspoon	0.5 milliliter
¼ teaspoon	1 milliliter
½ teaspoon	2 milliliters
1 teaspoon	5 milliliters
½ tablespoon	7 milliliters
1 tablespoon (3 teaspoons)	15 milliliters
2 tablespoons (1 fluid ounce)	30 milliliters
¼ cup (4 tablespoons)	60 milliliters
⊠ cup	90 milliliters
½ cup (4 fluid ounces)	125 milliliters
⊠ cup	160 milliliters
¾ cup (6 fluid ounces)	180 milliliters
1 cup (16 tablespoons)	250 milliliters
1 pint (2 cups)	500 milliliters
1 quart (4 cups)	1 liter (about)

WEIGHT CONVERSIONS	
U.S. Weight Measure	Metric Equivalent
½ ounce	15 grams
1 ounce	30 grams
2 ounces	60 grams
3 ounces	85 grams
¼ pound (4 ounces)	115 grams
½ pound (8 ounces)	225 grams
¾ pound (12 ounces)	340 grams
1 pound (16 ounces)	454 grams

OVEN TEMPERATURE CONVERSIONS	
Degrees Fahrenheit	Degrees Celsius
200 degrees F	95 degrees C
250 degrees F	120 degrees C
275 degrees F	135 degrees C
300 degrees F	150 degrees C
325 degrees F	160 degrees C
350 degrees F	180 degrees C
375 degrees F	190 degrees C
400 degrees F	205 degrees C
425 degrees F	220 degrees C
450 degrees F	230 degrees C

BAKING PAN SIZES	
U.S.	Metric
8 × 1½ inch round baking pan	20 × 4 cm cake tin
9 × 1½ inch round baking pan	23 × 3.5 cm cake tin
11 × 7 × 1½ inch baking pan	28 × 18 × 4 cm baking tin
13 × 9 × 2 inch baking pan	30 × 20 × 5 cm baking tin
2 quart rectangular baking dish	30 × 20 × 3 cm baking tin
15 × 10 × 2 inch baking pan	30 × 25 × 2 cm baking tin (Swiss roll tin)
9 inch pie plate	22 × 4 or 23 × 4 cm pie plate
7 or 8 inch springform pan	18 or 20 cm springform or loose bottom cake tin
9 × 5 × 3 inch loaf pan	23 × 13 × 7 cm or 2 lb narrow loaf or pâté tin
1½ quart casserole	1.5 liter casserole
2 quart casserole	2 liter casserole

INDEX